OUR
ELIZABETH

A Humour Novel

FLORENCE A. KILPATRICK

1st WORLD
LIBRARY
Literary Society

Our Elizabeth

Florence A. Kilpatrick

© 1st World Library, 2006
PO Box 2211
Fairfield, IA 52556
www.1stworldlibrary.com
First Edition

LCCN: 2006907679

Softcover ISBN: 1-4218-2424-8
Hardcover ISBN: 1-4218-2324-1
eBook ISBN: 1-4218-2524-4

Purchase *"Our Elizabeth"*
as a traditional bound book at:
www.1stWorldLibrary.com/purchase.asp?ISBN=1-4218-2424-8

1st World Library is a literary, educational organization
dedicated to:

- Creating a free internet library of downloadable ebooks

- Hosting writing competitions and offering book
  publishing scholarships.

Interested in more 1st World Library books?
contact: literacy@1stworldlibrary.com
Check us out at: www.1stworldlibrary.com

1ˢᵗ World Library Literary Society

Giving Back to the World

"If you want to work on the core problem, it's early school literacy."

- James Barksdale, former CEO of Netscape

"No skill is more crucial to the future of a child, or to a democratic and prosperous society, than literacy."

- Los Angeles Times

Literacy... means far more than learning how to read and write... The aim is to transmit... knowledge and promote social participation."

- UNESCO

"Literacy is not a luxury, it is a right and a responsibility. If our world is to meet the challenges of the twenty-first century we must harness the energy and creativity of all our citizens."

- President Bill Clinton

"Parents should be encouraged to read to their children, and teachers should be equipped with all available techniques for teaching literacy, so the varying needs and capacities of individual kids can be taken into account."

- Hugh Mackay

CHAPTER I

"PAUL!" The young man started, and a delicate flush mantled his handsome face, as he turned to the lady who had pronounced his name in a tone slightly indicative of surprise.

"Ah! Mrs. Denison," was his simple response.

"You seem unusually absent-minded this evening," remarked the lady.

"Do I?"

"Yes."

"You have been observing me?"

"I could not help it; for every time my eyes have wandered in this direction, they encountered you, standing in the same position, and looking quite as much like a statue as a living man."

"How long is it since I first attracted your attention?" inquired the person thus addressed, assuming an indifference of manner which it was plain he did not feel.

"If I were to say half an hour, it would not be far wide of the truth."

"Oh, no! It can't be five minutes since I came to this part of the room," said the young man, whose name was Paul Hendrickson. He seemed a little annoyed.

"Not a second less than twenty minutes," replied the lady. "Your thoughts must have been very busy thus to have removed nearly all ideas of time."

"They *were* busy," was the simple reply. But the low tones were full of meaning.

Mrs. Denison looked earnestly into her companion's face for several moments before venturing to speak farther. She then said, in a manner that showed her to be a privileged and warmly interested friend -

"Busy on what subject, Paul?"

The young man offered Mrs. Denison his arm, remarking as he did so -

"The other parlor is less crowded."

Threading their course amid the groups standing in gay conversation, or moving about the rooms, Paul Hendrickson and his almost maternal friend (sic) souhgt a more retired position near a heavily curtained window.

"You are hardly yourself to-night, Paul. How is it that your evenly balanced mind has suffered a disturbance. There must be something wrong within. You know my theory - that all disturbing causes are in the heart."

"I am not much interested in mental theories to-night - am in no philosophic mood. I feel too deeply for analysis."

"On what subject, Paul?"

A little while the young man sat with his eyes upon the floor; then lifting them to the face of Mrs. Denison, he replied.

T.S. Arthur

"You are not ignorant of the fact that Jessie Loring has interested me more than any maiden I have yet seen?"

"I am not, for you have already confided to me your secret."

"The first time I met her, it seemed to me as if I had come into the presence of one whose spirit claimed some hidden affinities with my own. I have never felt so strangely in the presence of a woman as I have felt and always feel in the presence of Miss Loring."

"She has a spirit of finer mould than most women," said Mrs. Denison. "I do not know her very intimately; but I have seen enough to give me a clue to her character. Her tastes are pure, her mind evenly balanced, and her intellect well cultivated."

"But she is only a woman."

Mr. Hendrickson sighed as he spoke.

"*Only* a woman! I scarcely understand you," said Mrs. Denison, gravely. "*I* am a woman."

"Yes, and a true woman! Forgive my words. They have only a conventional meaning," replied the young man earnestly.

"You must explain that meaning, as referring to Jessie Loring."

"It is this, only. She can be deceived by appearances. Her eyes are not penetrating enough to look through the tinsel and glitter with which wealth conceals the worthlessness of the man."

"Ah! you are jealous. There is a rival."

"You, alone, can use those words, and not excite my anger," said Hendrickson.

"Forgive me if they have fallen upon your ears unpleasantly."

"A rival, Mrs. Denison!" the young man spoke proudly. "That is something *I* will never have. The woman's heart that can warm under the smile of another man, is nothing to me."

"You are somewhat romantic, Paul, in your notions about matrimony. You forget that women are 'only' women."

"But I do *not* forget, Mrs. Denison, that as you have so often said to me, there are true marriages in which the parties are drawn towards each other by sexual affinities peculiar to themselves; and that a union in such cases, is the true union by which they become, in the language of inspiration, 'one flesh.' I can enter into none other. When I first met Jessie Loring, a spirit whispered to me - was it a lying spirit? - a spirit whispered to me - 'the beautiful complement of your life!' I believed on the instant. In that I may have been romantic."

"Perhaps not!" said Mrs. Denison.

Hendrickson looked into her face steadily for some moments, and then said -

"It was an illusion."

"Why do you say this, Paul? Why are you so disturbed? Speak your heart more freely."

"Leon Dexter is rich. I am - poor!"

"You are richer than Leon Dexter in the eyes of a true woman - richer a thousandfold, though he counted his wealth by millions." There were flashes of light in the eyes of Mrs. Denison.

Hendrickson bent his glance to the floor and did not reply.

"If Miss Loring prefers Dexter to you, let her move on in her way without a thought. She is not worthy to disturb, by even the shadow of her passing form, the placid current of your life.

T.S. Arthur

But I am by no means certain that he *is* preferred to you."

"He has been at her side all the evening," said the young man.

"That proves nothing. A forward, self-confident, agreeable young gentleman has it in his power thus to monopolize almost any lady. The really excellent, usually too modest, but superior young men, often permit themselves to be elbowed into the shade by these shallow, rippling, made up specimens of humanity, as you have probably done to-night."

"I don't know how that may be, Mrs. Denison; but this I know. I had gained a place by her side, early in the evening. She seemed pleased, I thought, at our meeting; but was reserved in conversation - too reserved it struck me. I tried to lead her out, but she answered my remarks briefly, and with what I thought an embarrassed manner. I could not hold her eyes - they fell beneath mine whenever I looked into her face. She was evidently ill at ease. Thus it was, when this self-confident Leon Dexter came sweeping up to us with his grand air, and carried her off to the piano. If I read her face and manner aright, she blessed her stars at getting rid of me so opportunely."

"I doubt if you read them aright," said Mrs. Denison, as her young friend paused. "You are too easily discouraged. If she is a prize, she is worth striving for. Don't forget the old adage - 'Faint heart never won fair lady.'"

Paul shook his head.

"I am too proud to enter the lists in any such contest," he answered. "Do you think I could beg for a lady's favorable regard? No! I would hang myself first!"

"How is a lady to know that you have a preference for her, if you do not manifest it in some way?" asked Mrs. Denison. "This is being a little too proud, my friend. It is throwing rather too much upon the lady, who must be wooed if she would be won."

"A lady has eyes," said Paul.

"Granted."

"And a lady's eyes can speak as well as her lips. If she likes the man who approaches her, let her say so with her eyes. She will not be misunderstood."

"You are a man," replied Mrs. Denison, a little impatiently; "and, from the beginning, man has not been able to comprehend woman! If you wait for a woman worth having to tell you, even with her eyes, that she likes you, and this before you have given a sign, you will wait until the day of doom. A true woman holds herself at a higher price!"

There was silence between the parties for the space of nearly a minute. Then Paul Hendrickson said -

"Few women can resist the attraction of gold. Creatures of taste - lovers of the beautiful - fond of dress, equipage, elegance - I do not wonder that we who have little beyond ourselves to offer them, find simple manhood light in the balance."

And he sighed heavily.

"It is because true men are not true to themselves and the true women Heaven wills to cross their paths in spring-time, that so many of them fail to secure the best for life-companions!" answered Mrs. Denison. "Worth is too retiring or too proud. Either diffidence or self-esteem holds it back in shadow. I confess myself to be sorely puzzled at times with the phenomenon. Why should the real man shrink away, and let the meretricious fop and the man 'made of money' win the beautiful and the best? Women are not such fools as to prefer tinsel to gold - the outside making up to the inner manhood! Neither are they so dim-sighted that they cannot perceive who is the man and who the 'fellow.' My word for it, if Miss

Loring's mind was known, you have a higher place therein than Dexter."

Just then the two persons of whom they were speaking passed near to them, Miss Loring on the arm of Dexter, her face radiant with smiles. He was saying something to which she was listening, evidently pleased with his remarks. The sight chafed the mind of Hendrickson, and he said, sarcastically -

"Like all the rest, Mrs. Denison! Gold is the magnet."

"You are in a strange humor to-night, Paul," answered his friend, "and your humor makes you unjust. It is not fair to judge Miss Loring in this superficial way. Because she is cheerful and social in a company like this, are you to draw narrow conclusions touching her heart-preferences?"

"Why was she not as cheerful and as social with me, as she is now with that fellow?" said the young man, a measure of indignation in the tones of his voice. "Answer me that, if you please."

"The true reason is, no doubt, wide of your conclusions," answered Mrs. Denison. "Genuine love, when it first springs to life in a maiden's heart, has in it a high degree of reverence. The object rises into something of superiority, and she draws near to it with repressed emotions, resting in its shadow, subdued, reserved, almost shy, but happy. She is not as we saw Miss Loring just now, but more like the maiden you describe as treating you not long ago with a strange reserve, which you imagined coldness."

"Woman is an enigma," exclaimed Hendrickson, his thoughts thrown into confusion.

"And you must study, if you would comprehend her," said Mrs. Denison. "Of one thing let me again assure you, my young friend, if you expect to get a wife worth having, you have got to show yourself in earnest. Other men, not half so worthy as you may be, have eyes quite as easily attracted by feminine loveliness, and they will press forward and rob you of the prize unless you put in a claim. A woman desires to be loved. Love is what her heart feeds upon, and the man who appears to love her best, even if in all things he is not her ideal of manhood, will be most apt to win her for his bride. You can win Miss Loring if you will."

"It may be so," replied the young man, almost gloomily. "But, for all you say, I must confess myself at fault. I look for a kind of spontaneity in love. It seems to me, that hearts, created to become one, should instinctively respond to each other. For this reason, the idea of wooing, and contending, and all that, is painfully repugnant."

"It may be," said Mrs. (sic) Dunham, "that your pride is as much at fault in the case, as your manhood. You cannot bend to solicit love."

"I cannot - I will not!" The gesture that accompanied this was as passionate as the surroundings would admit.

"It was pride that banished Lucifer from Heaven," said Mrs. Denison, "and I am afraid it will keep you out of the heaven of a true marriage here. Beware, my young friend! you are treading on dangerous ground. And there is, moreover, a consideration beyond your own case. The woman who can be happy in marriage with you, cannot be happy with another man. Let us, just to make the thing clear, suppose that Jessie Loring is the woman whose inner life is most in harmony with yours. If your lives blend in a true marriage, then will she find true happiness; but, if, through your failure to woo and win, she be drawn aside into a marriage with one whose life is inharmonious, to what a sad, weary, hopeless existence may she not be doomed. Paul! Paul! There are two aspects in which this question is to be viewed. I pray to Heaven that you may see it right."

Further conversation was prevented by the near approach

of others.

"Let me see you, and early, Paul," said Mrs. Denison. It was some hours later, and the company were separating. "I must talk with you again about Miss Loring."

Hendrickson promised to call in a day or two. As he turned from Mrs. Denison, his eyes encountered those of the young lady whose name had just been uttered. She was standing beside Mr. Dexter, who was officiously attentive to her up to the last moment. He was holding her shawl ready to throw it over her shoulders as she stepped from the door to the carriage that awaited her. For a moment or two the eyes of both were fixed, and neither had the power to move them. Then, each with a slight confusion of manner, turned from the other. Hendrickson retired into the nearly deserted parlors, while Miss Loring, attended by Dexter, entered the carriage, and was driven away.

CHAPTER II

IT was past the hour of two, when Jessie Loring stepped from the carriage and entered her home. A domestic admitted her.

"Aunt is not waiting for me?" she said in a tone of inquiry.

"No; she has been in bed some hours."

"It is late for you to be sitting up, Mary, and I am sorry to have been the cause of it. But, you know, I couldn't leave earlier."

She spoke kindly, and the servant answered in a cheerful voice.

"I'll sit up for you, Miss Jessie, at any time. And why shouldn't I? Sure, no one in the house is kinder or more considerate of us than you; and it's quite as little as a body can do to wait up for you once in a while, and you enjoying yourself."

"Thank you, Mary. And now get to bed as quickly as possible, for you must be tired and very sleepy. Good-night."

"Good night, and God bless you!" responded the servant, warmly. "She was the queen there, I know?" she added, proudly, speaking to herself as she moved away.

It was a night in mid-October. A clear, cool, moon-lit radiant night. From her window, Jessie could look far away over the housetops to a dark mass of forest trees, just beyond the city, and to the gleaming river that lay sleeping at their feet. The sky

T.S. Arthur

was cloudless, save at the west, where a tall, craggy mountain of vapor towered up to the very zenith. After loosening and laying off some of her garments, Miss Loring, instead (sic) off retiring, sat down by the window, and leaning her head upon her hand looked out upon the entrancing scene. She did not remark upon its beauty, nor think of its weird attractions; nor did her eyes, after the first glance, convey any distinct image of external objects to her mind. Yet was she affected by them. The hour, and the aspect of nature wrought their own work upon her feelings.

She sat down and leaned her head upon her hand, while the scenes in which she had been for the past few hours an actor, passed before her in review with almost the vividness of reality. Were her thoughts pleasant ones? We fear not; for every now and then a faint sigh troubled her breast, and parted her too firmly closed lips. The evening's entertainment had not satisfied her in something. There was a pressure on her feelings that weighed them down heavily.

"There is more in one sentence of his than in a a page of the other's wordy utterances." Her lips moved in the earnestness of her inward-spoken thoughts. "How annoyed I was to be dragged from his side by Mr. Dexter just as I had begun to feel a little at my ease, and just as my voice had gained something of its true expression. It is strange how his presence disturbs me; and how my eyes fall beneath his gaze! He seems very cold and very distant; and proud I should think. Proud! Ah! has he not cause for pride? I have not looked upon his peer to-night. How that man did persecute me with his attentions! He monopolized me wholly! Perhaps I should be flattered by his attentions - and, perhaps, I was. I know that I was envied. Ah, me! what a pressure there is on my heart! From the moment I first looked into the face of Paul Hendrickson, I have been an enigma to myself. Some great change is wrought in me - some new capacities opened - some deeper yearnings quickened into life. I am still Jessie Loring, though not the Jessie Loring of yesterday. Have I completed a cycle of being? Am I entering upon another and higher sphere of existence? How the questions bewilder me! Clouds and darkness seem gathering around me, and my heart springs upward, half in fear, and half in hope!"

An hour later, and Miss Loring still sat by the closed window, her eyes upon the gleaming river and sombre woods beyond, yet seeing them not. The tall mountain of vapor, which had arisen like a pyramid of white marble, no longer retained its clear, bold outline, but, yielding to aerial currents, had been rent from base to crown, and now its scattered fragments lay in wild confusion along the whole sweep of the western horizon. Down into these shapeless ruins the moon had plunged, and her pure light was struggling to penetrate their rifts, and pour its blessing upon the slumbering earth.

A rush of wind startled the maiden from her deep abstraction, and, as it went moaning away among the eaves and angles of the surrounding tenements, she arose, and putting off her garments, went sighing to bed. Dreams visited her in sleep, and in every dream she was in the presence of Paul Hendrickson. Very pleasant were they, for in the sweet visions that came to her, Paul was by her side, his voice filling her ears and echoing in her heart like tones of delicious music. They walked through fragrant meadows, by the side of glittering streams, and amid groves with singing birds on all the blossomy branches. How tenderly he spoke to her! - how reverently he touched with his manly lips her soft white hand, sending such electric thrills of joy to her heart as waking maidens rarely know! But, suddenly, after a long season of blessed intercourse, a stern voice shocked her ears, and a heavy hand grasped roughly her arm. She turned in fear, and Leon Dexter stood before her, a dark frown upon his countenance. With a cry of terror she awoke.

Day had already come, but no bright sun shone down upon the earth, for leaden clouds were in the sky, and nature was bathed in tears. It was some time before the agitation that accompanied Miss Loring's sudden awakening, had sufficiently subsided to leave her mind composed enough to arise and join

T.S. Arthur

the family. When she did so, she found her aunt, Mrs. Loring and her cousins Amanda and Dora, two not over refined school girls, aged fourteen and sixteen, awaiting her appearance.

"You are late this morning, Jessie," said Mrs. Loring. Then, before her niece had time to reply, she spoke to her eldest daughter - "Amanda, ring the bell, and order breakfast at once."

"I am sorry to have kept you waiting, aunt Phoebe," replied Jessie. "I did not get to bed until very late, and slept too soundly for the morning bell."

"You must have been as deeply buried in the arms of Morpheus as one of the seven sleepers, not to have heard that bell! I thought Kitty would never stop the intolerable din. The girl seems to have a passion for bell-ringing. Her last place was, I fancy, a boarding-house."

Mrs. Loring spoke with a slight shade of annoyance in her tones. Her words and manner, it was plain from Jessie's countenance, were felt as a rebuke. In a few moments the breakfast bell was heard, and the family went down to the morning meal, which had been delayed full half an hour beyond the usual time.

"Had you a pleasant time last evening?" inquired Mrs. Loring, after they were seated at the table, and a taste of the fragrant coffee and warm cakes had somewhat refreshed her body, and restored the tranquillity of her feelings.

"Very," replied Jessie in an absent way.

"Who was there?"

"Oh! everybody. It was a very large company."

"Who in particular that I know?"

"Mrs. Compton and her daughter Agnes."

"Indeed! Was Agnes there?" said Mrs. Loring, in manifest surprise.

"Yes; and she looked beautiful."

"I didn't know that she had come out. Agnes must be very young - not over seventeen. I am surprised at her mother! How did she behave herself? Bold, forward and hoydenish enough, I suppose! I never liked her."

"I did not observe any impropriety of conduct," said Jessie. "She certainly was neither bold nor forward."

"Did she sing?"

"No."

"Probably no one asked her." Mrs. Loring was in a cynical mood.

"Yes; I heard her asked more than once to sing."

"And she refused?"

"Yes."

"Affectation! She wanted urging. She has had peculiar advantages, and is said to possess fine musical ability. I have heard that she is a splendid performer. No doubt she was dying to show off at the piano."

"I think not," said Jessie, "for I heard her say to Mrs. Compton, in an under tone, 'I can't, indeed, dear mother! The very thought of playing before these people, makes my heart tremble. I can play very well at home, when my mind is calm; but I should blunder in the first bar here.'"

T.S. Arthur

"Children should be left at home," said Mrs. Loring. "That is my doctrine. This crowding of young girls into company, and crowding out grown up people, is a great mistake; but, who else was there? What gentlemen?"

"Mr. Florence."

Mrs. Loring curled her flexible lip.

"Mr. Dexter."

"Leon?"

"Yes."

The eyes of Jessie drooped as those of her aunt were directed in close scrutiny to her face.

"He's a catch. Set your cap for him, Jessie, and you may ride in your own carriage." There was a vulgar leer in Mrs. Loring's eye. The color rose to Jessie's face, but she did not answer.

"Did he show you any attentions?" inquired the aunt.

"Yes. He was quite as attentive as I could desire."

"Indeed! And what does 'as you could desire,' mean?"

Jessie turned her face partly away to hide its crimson.

"Ah, well; I see how it is, dear. You needn't blush so. I only hope you may get him. He was attentive, then, was he?"

"I have no reason to complain of his lack of attentions, said Jessie, her voice cold and firm. "They would have been flattering to most girls. But, I do not always give to compliments and 'company manners,' the serious meanings that some attach to them."

"Jessie," Mrs. Loring spoke with sudden seriousness; "take my advice, and encourage Leon Dexter. I am pleased to know that you were so much an object of his attentions as your remarks lead me to infer. I know that you will make him a good wife; one of whom he can never be ashamed; and I know that a union with him will give you a proud position."

"Will you waive the subject, at present, dear aunt?" said Jessie, with a pleading look, at the same time glancing covertly towards her cousins, who were drinking in every word with girlish eagerness.

"Oh, by all means," answered Mrs. Loring, "if it is in the least annoying. I was forgetting myself in the interest felt for your welfare."

"And so Mr. Dexter showed you marked attentions last evening?" said Jessie's aunt, joining her in the sitting-room, after Amanda and Dora had left for school.

"Did I say so, aunt?" inquired Jessie, looking into her relative's face.

"You said enough to make the inference clear, my child."

"Well, Aunt Phoebe, he was attentive - more so, by a great deal, than I desired!"

"Than you desired!" There was unfeigned surprise in the voice of Mrs. Loring. "What do you mean, Jessie?"

"The man's position is all well enough; but the man himself is not altogether to my liking."

"You must have grown remarkably fastidious all at once. Why, girl! there isn't a handsomer man to be found anywhere. He is a noble looking fellow! Where are your eyes?"

"The man that a wife has to deal with, is the man of the spirit,

Aunt Phoebe - the real man. The handsome outside is nothing, if the inner man is not beautiful!" Jessie spoke with a sudden glow of feeling.

"Stuff and nonsense, child!" said Mrs. Loring, impatiently. "Stuff and nonsense!" she repeated, seeing that her niece looked steadily into her face. "What do you know of the man of the spirit, as you call it? And, moreover, what possesses you to infer that Mr. Dexter's inner man is not as beautiful as the outer?"

"The soul looks forth from the eyes, and manifests its quality in the tones of the voice," replied Jessie, a fine enthusiasm illuminating her beautiful face. "No man can hide from us his real character, unless we let self-love and self-interest draw an obscuring veil."

"You are a strange girl, Jessie - a very strange girl!" Mrs. Loring was fretted. "What can you mean? Here, a splendid fortune promises to be poured into your lap, and you draw your garments aside, hesitating and questioning as to whether the golden treasure is worth receiving! I am half amazed at your conduct!"

"Are you weary of my presence here, Aunt Phoebe?" said Jessie, a tremor in her low failing tones.

"Now give me patience with the foolish girl!" exclaimed Mrs. Loring, assuming an angry aspect. "What has come over you, Jessie? Did I say anything about being wearied with your presence? Because I manifest an unusual degree of interest in your future welfare, am I to be charged with a mean, selfish motive? I did not expect this of you."

"Dear aunt! forgive me!" said Jessie, giving way to tears. "My feelings are unusually disturbed this morning. Late hours and the excitement of company have made me nervous. As for Mr. Dexter, let us pass him by for the present. He has not impressed me as favorably as you seem to desire."

"But Jessie."

"Spare me, dear aunt! If you press the subject on me now, you will only excite disgust where you hope to create a favorable impression. I have had many opportunities of close observation, and failed not to improve them. The result is"

Jessie paused.

"What?" queried her aunt.

"That the more narrowly I scan him the less I like him. He is superficial, vain and selfish."

"How do you know?"

"I cannot make manifest to your eyes the signs that were clear to mine. But so I have read him."

"And read him with the page upside down, my, word for it, Miss Jessie Loring!"

Jessie answered only with a sigh, and when her aunt still pressed her on the subject, she begged to be spared, as she felt nervous and excited. So, leaving the sitting room, she retired to her own apartment, to gather up, and unravel, if possible, the tangled thread of thought and feeling.

CHAPTER III

"THERE is a gentleman in the parlor, Miss Jessie," said Mary, the chambermaid, opening the door and presenting her plain, but pleasant face. It was an hour after Miss Loring had left her aunt in the sitting room.

"Who is it, Mary?"

The girl handed her a card.

On it was engraved, PAUL HENDRICKSON. The heart of Jessie Loring gave a sudden leap, and the blood sprung reddening to her very temples.

"Say that I will be with him in a few minutes."

The servant retired, and Jessie, who had arisen as she received the card, sat down, so overcome by her feelings, that she felt all bodily strength depart.

"Paul Hendrickson!" she said, whispering the name. "How little did I expect a visit from him! After our first interview last evening, he seemed studiously to avoid me."

Then she arose hastily, but in a tremor, and made some hurried changes in her dress. She was about leaving her room, when Mary again presented herself.

"Another gentleman has called," and she handed another card.

Jessie took it and read LEON DEXTER!

Could anything have been more inopportune! Jessie felt a double embarrassment.

"The fates are against me I believe!" she murmured, as, after a few moments of vigorous expression of feeling, she left her room, and descended to the parlor, entering with a light but firm tread. Dexter stepped quickly forward, giving his hand in the most assured style, and putting both her and himself entirely at ease. She smiled upon him blandly, because she felt the contagion of his manner. Hendrickson was more formal and distant, and showed some embarrassment. He was not at ease himself, and failed to put Jessie at ease.

After all were seated, Dexter talked freely, while Hendrickson sat, for the most part silent, but, as Jessie felt, closely observant. Light and playful were the subjects introduced by Mr. Dexter, and his remarks caused a perpetual ripple of smiles to sparkle over the countenance of Miss Loring. But whenever Mr. Hendrickson spoke to her, the smiles faded, and she turned upon him a face so changed in expression that he felt a chill pervade his feelings. She did not mean to look grave; she did not repress the smiles purposely; there was neither coldness nor repulsion in her heart. But her sentiments touching Mr. Hendrickson were so different from those entertained for Mr. Dexter; and her estimation of his character so widely variant that she could not possibly treat him with the smiling familiarity shown towards the other. Yet all the while she was painfully conscious of being misunderstood. If she had met Mr. Hendrickson alone, she felt that it must have been different. A degree of embarrassment might have existed, but she would not have been forced to put on two opposite exteriors, as now, neither of which, correctly interpreted her state of mind, or did justice to her character.

"I did not see much of you last evening, Mr. Hendrickson. What were you doing with yourself?" she remarked, trying to be more familiar, and giving him a look that set his pulses to a quicker measure. Before he could answer, Dexter said, gaily, yet with covert sarcasm.

"Oh, Mr. Hendrickson prefers the society of elderly ladies. He spent the evening in sober confabulation with Mrs. Denison. I have no doubt she was edified. *I* prefer maid to matron, at any time. Old women are my horror."

Too light and gay were the tones of Dexter to leave room for offence. Hendrickson tried to rally himself, and retort with pleasant speech. But his heart was too deeply interested, - and his mood too serious for sport. His smile did not improve the aspect of his countenance; and if he meant his words for witticisms, they were perceived as sarcasms. Jessie was rather repelled than attracted - all of which he saw.

Conscious that he was wholly misrepresenting himself in the young lady's eyes, and feeling, moreover, that he was only spoiling pleasant company, Hendrickson, after a brief call, left the field clear to his rival. Jessie accompanied him to the door.

"I shall be pleased to see you again, Mr. Hendrickson," she said, in a tone of voice that betrayed something of her interest in him.

He turned to look into her eyes. They sustained his penetrating gaze only for a moment and then her long lashes lay upon her crimsoning cheeks.

"Not if I show myself as stupid as I have been this morning," said the young man.

"I have never thought you stupid, Mr. Hendrickson."

"I am dull at times," he said, hesitating, and slightly confused. "Good morning!" he added, abruptly, and turned off without another look into the eyes that were upon him; and in which he would have read more than his heart had dared to hope for.

"What a boor!" exclaimed Dexter as Miss Loring returned to the parlor.

"Oh, no, not a boor, sir. Far, very far from that," answered the young lady promptly.

"Well, you don't call him a gentleman, do you?"

"I have seen nothing that would rob him of the title," said Miss Loring.

"A true gentleman will put on a gentlemanly exterior; for he is courteous by instinct - and especially when ladies are present. A true gentleman, moreover, is always at his ease. Self-possession is one of the signs of a well bred man. Hendrickson is not well bred. Any one who has been at all in society, can perceive this at a glance. Did you notice how he played with his watch chain; crossed his legs in sitting; took out his pencil case, and moved the slide noisily backwards and forwards; ran his fingers through his hair; exhibited his pocket-handkerchief half-a-dozen times in as many minutes, and went through sundry other performances of which no well bred man is guilty? I marvel, that a young lady of your refinement can offer a word of apology for such things. I see in it only kindness of heart; and this shall be your excuse."

So gaily were the closing sentences uttered; yet with so manifest a regard softening the final words, that Miss Loring's rising anger against the young man, went down and was extinguished in a pleasing consciousness of being an object of marked favor by one whose external attractions, at least, were of the highest order.

"But the subject is not agreeable to either of us, Miss Loring," said Dexter in a voice pitched to a lower tone, and with a softer modulation. "I did not expect to find a visitor here at so early an hour; and I fear that I have permitted myself to experience just a shade of annoyance. If I have seemed ill-natured, pardon me. It is not my nature to find fault, or to

T.S. Arthur

criticise. I rather prefer looking upon the bright side. Like Sir Joshua Reynolds, 'I am a wide liker.' There are times, you know, in which we are all tempted to act in a way that gives to others a false impression of our real characters."

"No one is more conscious of that than I am," replied Miss Loring. "Indeed, it seems often, as if I were made the sport of adverse influences, and constrained to act and to appear wholly different from what I desire to seem. There are some of life's phenomena, Mr. Dexter, that puzzle at times my poor brain sorely."

"Don't puzzle over such things, Miss Loring," said Mr. Dexter; "I never do. Leave mysteries to philosophers; there is quite enough of enjoyment upon the surface of things without diving below, into the dark caverns of doubt and vague speculation. I never liked the word phenomenon."

"To me it has ever been an attraction. I always seem standing at some closed door, hearkening to vague sounds within and longing to enter. The outer life presents itself to me as moving figures in a show, and I am all impatient, at times, to discover the hidden machinery that gives such wonderful motion.

"Morbid; all morbid!" answered Dexter, in a lively manner. "Dreams in the place of realities, Miss Loring. Don't philosophize; don't speculate; don't think - at least not seriously. Your thinkers are always miserable. Take life as it is - full of beauty, full of pleasure. The sources of enjoyment are all around us. Let us drink at them and be thankful."

"You are a philosopher, I perceive," said Miss Loring, with a smile, "and must have been a thinker, in some degree, to have formed a theory."

"I am a cheerful philosopher."

"Are you always cheerful, Mr. Dexter?" inquired Miss Loring.

"Always."

"Never feel the pressure of gloomy states? Have no transitions of feeling - sudden, unaccountable; as if the shadow of a cloud had fallen over your spirit?"

"Never."

"You are singularly fortunate."

"Am I, Miss Loring?" and the young man's voice grew tender as he leaned nearer to the maiden.

"I am blessed with a cheerful temper," he added, "and I cultivate the inheritance. It is a good gift - blessing both the inheritor and his companions. Neither men nor women are long gloomy in my presence."

"I have often noticed your smiling face and pleasant words," said Jessie, "and wondered if you moved always in a sunny atmosphere."

"You are answered now," he replied.

A little while there was silence. Jessie did not feel the repulsion which had at first made Dexter's presence annoying; and as he drew his chair closer, and leaned still nearer, there was on her part no instinctive receding.

"Yes," she murmured softly, almost dreamily, "I am answered."

"Jessie." The young man's breath was on her cheek - his hand touching her hand. She remained sitting very still - still as an effigy.

"Jessie." How very low, and loving, and musical was the voice that thrilled along the chords of feeling! "Jessie; forgive me if I have mistaken the signs." His hand tightened upon hers. She felt spell-bound. She wished to start up and flee. But she could not. There was a strange, overshadowing, half paralyzing power in the man's presence. Without a purpose to do so, she returned the pressure of his hand. It was enough.

"Thanks, dear one!" he murmured. "I was sure I had not mistaken the signs. The heart has language all its own."

Still the maiden's form was motionless; and her hand lay passive in the hand that now held it with a strong clasp. Yet, how wildly did her heart beat! How tumultuous were all her feelings! How delicious the thrill that pervaded her being!

"I love you, Jessie! Dear one! Angel! And by this token you are mine!" said Dexter, his voice full of passion's fine enthusiasm. And he raised her hand to his lips, kissing it half-wildly as he did so.

"The gods have made this hour propitious!" he added, as he drew her head down against his bosom, and laid his ardent lips to hers. "Bless you, darling! Bless you!" he went on. "My life is crowned this hour with its chiefest delight! Mine! mine!"

Yet, not a word had parted the maiden's lips, thus spirited away, as it were, out of herself, and strangely betrayed into consenting silence. She had neither given her yea nor her nay - and dared as little to speak the one as the other.

Almost bereft of (sic) physical power, she sat with her face hidden on the bosom of this impulsive lover, for many minutes. At last, thought cleared itself a little, and, with a more distinct self-consciousness, were restored individuality and strength. She raised herself, moved back a little, and looked up into the face of Mr. Dexter. The aspect of her own was not just what the young man had expected to see. He did not look upon a countenance blushing in sweet confusion; nor into eyes radiant with loving glances; but upon a pale face, and eyes whose meanings were a mystery. Slowly, yet persistently, did she withdraw her hand from his clasp, while slowly her form arose, until it gained an erect position.

"You have taken me off my guard, Mr. Dexter," she said, a tremor running through her voice.

"Say not a word, Jessie! say not a word! I am only too happy to have taken your heart captive. You are none the less my own, whether the means were force or stratagem."

"Speak not too confidently, sir. Have I" -

Mr. Dexter raised his hand quickly, and uttered a word of warning. But were silent again. Then the young man said, his manner growing deferential, and his voice falling to a low and subdued tone -

"Miss Loring, I here offer you heart and hand; and in making this offer, do most solemnly affirm that you are precious to me as life. - The highest boon I can crave from heaven is the gift of your dear self."

As he spoke, he extended his hand towards her. But her own did not stir from her lap, where it lay as still as if paralyzed.

"This is no light matter, Mr. Dexter," she said; still with the huskiness and tremor which had before veiled her voice. "I cannot decide on a thing of such infinite moment, in hot blood and on the spur of a sudden occasion. You must give me time for reflection."

"The heart knows no time. It neither reasons nor deliberates; but speaks out upon the instant, as yours has already done, Miss Loring," replied Dexter, with reviving ardor.

"Time, Mr. Dexter, time! I must have time!" said Jessie, almost imploringly.

But Dexter, who saw that time might turn the scale against him, resolved to press his suit then to the final issue.

"I cannot accept delay," he answered, throwing the most

winning tenderness into his voice. "And why should you hesitate a moment?"

"My aunt" - murmured Jessie.

"Consult her with all maidenly formality. That is right - that is prudent," he said, leaning again very near to her. "But, ere we separate this morning, let me ask one question - I am not disagreeable to you?"

"Oh, no, no, Mr. Dexter!" was the quick, earnest reply.

"Nor is your heart given to another?"

"No lips but yours have ever uttered such words as have sounded in my ears this day."

"And no lips, speaking in your ears, can ever utter such words with half the heart-warmth that were in mine, dear Jessie! True love is ever ardent, and cannot wait. I must have a sign from you before I leave. You need not speak; but lay your hand in mine," and he reached his hand towards her.

It was a moment of strong trial. Again her thoughts fell into confusion. Again a wild delicious thrill swept like a strain of music through all her being. She was within the sphere of an irresistible attraction. Her hand fluttered with a sudden impulse, and then, moving towards the hand of Dexter, was seized and covered with kisses.

"Thanks, dearest!" he murmured. "Thanks! By this token I know that I am loved - by this token you are mine - mine forever! Happy, happy day! It shall be the golden one in all the calendar of my life."

With the ardor of passion he drew her to his side again, and clasping his arm around her, kissed her with all the fervor of an entranced lover - kissed her over and over again, wildly.

All this was not mere acting on the part of Mr. Dexter. He did love the sweet young girl as truly as men of his peculiar character are capable of loving. He was deeply in earnest. There was a charm about Jessie Loring which had captivated him in the beginning. She was endowed with rich mental gifts, as well as personal beauty; and with both, Dexter was charmed even to fascination. Superficial, vain of his person, and self-satisfied from his position, he had not been much troubled by doubts touching his ability to secure the hand of Miss Loring, and by his very boldness and ardor, won his suit ere she had sufficient warning of his purpose to throw a mail-clad garment around her.

Dexter remained for only a short period after this ardent declaration. He had penetration enough to see that Miss Loring was profoundly disturbed, and that she desired to be alone. He saw with concern that her countenance was losing its fine warmth, and that the lustre of her eyes was failing. Her look was becoming more inverted each moment. She was trying to read her heart, and understand the writing inscribed thereon.

"I will see you this evening, Jessie," said Mr. Dexter, on rising to depart. Their intercourse had already been touched with a shade of embarrassment.

Miss Loring forced a smile and simply inclined her head. He bent forward and kissed her. Passively - almost coldly was the salute received. Then they parted. A film of ice had already formed itself between them.

CHAPTER IV

ON leaving Mr. Dexter, Jessie Loring almost flew to her room, like one escaping from peril. Closing and locking the door, she crossed the apartment, and falling forward against the bed, sunk down upon her knees and buried her face in a pillow. She did not pray. There was no power in her to lift a petition upwards. But weak, in bewilderment of spirit and abandonment of will she bent in deep prostration of soul and body.

It was nearly an hour before she arose. Very calm had her mind become in this long interval - very calm and very clear. With the plummet line of intense thought, quickened by keen perception, she had sounded the depths of her heart. She found places there - capacities for loving - intense yearnings - which had remained hidden until now. The current of her life had hitherto run smoothly in the sunshine, its surface gleaming and in breezy ripples. But the stream had glided from the open meadows and the sunshine, and the shadow of a great rock had fallen upon it. The surface was still as glass; and now looking downward, she almost shuddered as sight descended away, away into bewildering depths. She held her breath as she gazed like one suspended in mid-air.

"Too late! too late!" she murmured, as she lifted herself up. "Too late!"

Her countenance was pale, even haggard. There was no color in her lips - her eyes were leaden - her aspect like one who had been shocked with the news of a great calamity.

Mrs. Loring, Jessie's aunt, had been informed by the servant of whom she made inquiry, as to the identity of the gentleman who had called that morning to see her niece - or at least as to the identity of one of them. She did not make out by the servant's description the personality of Mr. Hendrickson, but that of Mr. Dexter was clear enough. She was also informed that the one whose name she could not guess, made only a brief visit, and that Mr. Dexter remained long, and was for most of the time in earnest conversation with Jessie. Her hopes gave her conclusions a wide latitude. She doubted not that the elegant, wealthy suitor was pressing a claim for the hand of her niece.

"Will she be such a little fool as to throw this splendid chance away?" she questioned with herself. "No - no;" was the answer. "Jessie will not dare to do it! She is a strange girl in some things, and wonderfully like her mother; but she will never refuse Leon Dexter, if so lucky as to get an offer."

Mrs. Loring heard Mr. Dexter leave the house, and with expectation on tip-toe, waited for Jessie to join her in the sitting-room. But while she yet listened for the sound of footsteps on the stairs below, her ears caught the light rustle of Jessie's garment as she glided along the passages and away to her own chamber.

"Something has taken place!" said Mrs. Loring to herself. "There's been a proposal, I'll bet my life on't! Why didn't the girl come and tell me at once? Ain't I her nearest relative - and haven't I always been like an own mother to her? But she's so peculiar - just as Alice used to be. I don't believe I shall ever understand her."

And Mrs. Loring fretted a little in her moderate way, not being capable of any very profound emotion. Ten, fifteen, twenty minutes - half an hour she waited for Jessie to appear. But there was no movement in the neighborhood of her chamber.

T.S. Arthur

"Didn't Jessie go to her room, after the gentleman went away?" asked Mrs. Loring, speaking to a servant, who was passing down the stairs.

"Yes, ma'am."

"Is she there now?"

"I believe so ma'am. I haven't seen her anywhere about the house."

The servant passed on, and Mrs. Loring waited for full half an hour longer. Then, unable to repress impatient curiosity, she went to Jessie's room and knocked at the door. Twice she knocked before there was a sound of life within. Then she heard footsteps - a bolt was withdrawn, and the door opened.

"Jessie!" exclaimed Mrs. Loring, "how white you are! What has happened?"

"Come in dear aunt!" said Jessie, "I have been wanting to see you; but had not yet made up my mind to seek you in the sitting-room. I am glad you are here."

Mrs. Loring passed in and Jessie closed the door.

"Take this seat aunt," and she pointed to an easy-chair: "I will sit here," drawing a lower one close to that which Mrs. Loring had taken.

"Now, dear, what has happened?" Mrs. Loring's curiosity had been so long upon the stretch, that she could ill endure delay.

"Will you listen to me patiently, Aunt Phoebe?"

There was a calmness of manner about Jessie that seemed to Mrs. Loring unnatural.

"Speak, dear - you will find me all attention."

"I am in a - strait. I must act; but cannot of my own reason, determine what action is right," said Jessie, "you must think for me, and help me to a just decision."

"Go on dear," urged Mrs. Loring.

Then as briefly and as clearly as possible, Jessie related all that had passed in her excited interview with Mr. Dexter. On concluding, she said with much earnestness of manner:

"And now, Aunt Phoebe, what I wish to know is this - will Mr. Dexter be warranted in regarding either my words or my actions, as an acceptance of his offer?"

"Certainly," was the unhesitating reply of Mrs. Loring.

"Aunt Phoebe!"

There was a tone of anguish in the voice of Jessie; and her pale lips grew paler.

"Why, what can ail you, child?" said Mrs. Loring.

"I had hoped for a different decision. Mr. Dexter took me at unawares. In a certain sense, I was mesmerized by the stronger action of his mind, quickened by an ardent temperament. Self-consciousness was for a time lost, and I moved and acted by the power of his will. There was no consentation in the right meaning of the word, Aunt Phoebe, and I cannot think I am bound."

"Bound, fully, in word and act Jessie," was Mrs. Loring's firmly spoken answer. "And so every one will regard you. Mr. Dexter, I am sure, will not admit your interpretation for an instant. He, it is plain, looks upon you as affianced. So do I!"

"Oh, aunt! aunt!" cried Jessie, clasping her hands, "say not so! say not so! Knowing, as you do, all that occurred, even to the utmost particulars of my strange position in the interview, how can you take part against me?"

"Take part against you, (sic) clild! How strangely you talk! One who did not know Mr. Dexter, might suppose him to be an Ogre, or second Blue Beard. I think the events of this morning the most fortunate of your life."

"While I fear they will prove most disastrous," said Jessie.

"Nonsense, child! you are excited and nervous. There is always something novel and romantic to a young girl in an offer of marriage. It (sic) it the great event of her life. I do not wonder that you are disturbed - though I am surprised at the nature of this disturbance. Time will subdue all this. You have a beautiful life before you, darling! The cherished bride of Leon Dexter must tread a path of roses."

A long sigh parted the lips of Miss Loring, and her face, to which not even the faintest tinge of color had yet returned, bent itself downward. She was silent.

"You leaned your face against him?" said Mrs. Loring.

"He drew my head down. I had no power of resistance, aunt. There was a spell upon my senses."

"You did not reject his ardent kisses?"

"I could not."

"And when he extended his hand, and asked you to lay your own within it, as a sign and a token of love, you gave him the sign and the token. Your hands clasped in a covenant of the heart! So he regarded the act. So do I; and so will all the world regard it. Jessie, the die is cast. You cannot retreat without dishonor."

"Will you leave me, aunt?" said Jessie, after a long silence. Her tones were sad. "I am very much excited. All this has unnerved me. I would like to be alone again."

"Better come down into the sitting-room," replied Mrs. Loring.

"No, aunt. You must let me have my way."

"Willful, and like your mother," said Mrs. Loring, as she arose.

"Was my mother willful?" inquired Jessie, looking at her aunt.

"Sometimes."

"Was she happy?"

"No. I do not think she ever understood or rightly appreciated your father. But, I should not have said this. She was a beautiful, fascinating young creature, as I remember her, and your father was crazy to get her. But I don't think they were very happy together. Where the blame lay I never knew for certain, and I will make no suggestions now."

"They were uncongenial in their tastes, perhaps," said Jessie.

"Dear knows what the reason was! But she died young, poor thing! and your father was in a sad way about it. I thought, of course, he would marry again. But he did not - living a widower until his death."

"Is my mother's picture very much like her, Aunt Phoebe?"

"Very like her; but not so handsome."

"She was beautiful?"

"Oh, yes; and the reigning belle before her marriage."

Jessie questioned no farther. Her aunt's recollections of her mother were all too external to satisfy the yearnings of her

T.S. Arthur

heart towards that mother. Often had she sat gazing upon the picture which represented to her eyes the form and face of a parent she had never seen; and sought to comprehend some of the meanings in the blue orbs that looked down upon her so calmly. But ever had she turned awaywith vague, unquiet, restless feelings.

"If my mother had lived!" she would sometimes say to herself, "she could comprehend me. Into her ears I could speak words that now sleep on my lips in perpetual silence.

"Oh, if my mother were alive!" sobbed the unhappy girl, as the door closed on the retiring form of wordly-minded Aunt Phoebe. "If my mother were only alive!

"Affianced!" she said a little while after, as thought went back to the interview between herself and Mrs. Loring which had just closed. "Affianced! Yes, that was the word. 'He regards you as affianced, and so do I!' How completely has this web invested me! Is there no way of escape?" A slight shudder went through her frame. "Ah, well, well!" - low and mournfully - "It may be that my woman's ideal has been too exalted, and above the standard of real men. Mr. Dexter is handsome; kind-hearted enough, no doubt; moderately well cultivated; rich, elegant in manner, though a little too demonstrative; and, most to be considered, loves me - or, at least, declares himself my lover. That he is sincere I cannot doubt. His was not the role of a skillful actor, but living expression. I ought to be flattered if not won by the homage he pays me."

Then she sat down, and began looking into her heart again, her keen vision penetrating to its farthest recesses. A long fluttering sigh breathed at length through her lips, and starting up she said,

"I am weak and foolish! Life is a reality; not a cycle of dreamy romance. All poetry lies in the dim distance - a thing of memory or anticipation - the present is invariably prose. How these vague ideals do haunt the mind! Love! Love! I had imagined something deeper, purer, holier than anything stirring in my heart for Leon Dexter! Was I deceived? Is the poet's song but jingling rhyme? - a play of words in trancing measure? Let me bind back into quie tudethese wildly leaping impulses, and clip the wings of these girlish fancies. They lead not the soul to happiness in a world like ours."

Again her form drooped, and again she sat for a long period so lost in the mazes of her own thoughts, that time and place receded alike from her consciousness. Not until dinner-time did she join her aunt. Her cousins had returned from school, and she met them as usual at the table. Her exterior was carefully controlled, so that the only change visible was a slight pallor and a graver aspect. Mrs. Loring scrutinized her countenance closely. This she bore without a sign of embarrassment. She partook but lightly of food. After the meal closed she retired to her own room, once more to torture her brain in a fruitless effort to solve this great problem of her life.

T.S. Arthur

CHAPTER V

WHEN Paul Hendrickson left the house of Mrs. Loring, his mind was in a state of painful excitement. The inopportune appearance of Dexter had so annoyed him, that he had found it impossible to assume the easy, cheerful air of a visitor. He was conscious, therefore, of having shown himself in the eyes of Miss Loring to very poor advantage. Her manner at parting had, however, reassured him. As they stood for a moment in the vestibule he saw her in a new light. The aspect of her countenance was changed, the eyes, that fell beneath his earnest gaze, burned with a softened light, and he read there a volume of tender interest at a single glance.

"I shall be pleased to see you again, Mr. Hendrickson." There was more than a parting compliment in her tones as she said these words. "I have never thought you stupid." What pleasure he derived from repeating these sentences over and over again! Early in the evening he called upon his friend Mrs. Denison.

"I have come to talk with you again about Miss Loring," said he. "I can't get her out of my thoughts. Her presence haunts me like a destiny."

Mrs. Denison smiled as she answered a little playfully:

"A genuine case of love; the infection taken at first sight. Isn't it so, Paul?"

"That I love this girl, in spite of myself, is, I fear, a solemn fact," said the young man, with an expression of face that did not indicate a very agreeable self-consciousness.

"Fear? In spite of yourself? A solemn fact? What a contradiction you are, Paul!" said Mrs. Denison.

"A man in love is an enigma. I have often heard it remarked, and I now perceive the saying to be true. I am an enigma. Yes, I love this girl in spite of myself; and the fact is a solemn one. Why? Because I have too good reason for believing that she does not love me in return. And yet, even while I say this, tones and words of hers, heard only to-day, come sighing to my ears, giving to every heart-beat a quicker impulse."

"Ah! Then you have seen Miss Loring to-day?"

"Yes," answered Hendrickson, in a quick, and suddenly excited manner. "I called upon her this morning, and while I sat in the parlor awaiting her appearance, who should intrude himself but that fellow Dexter. I felt like annihilating him. The look I gave him he will remember."

"That was bad taste, Paul," said Mrs. Denison.

"I know it. But his appearance was so untimely; and then, I had not forgotten last evening. The fellow has a world of assurance; and he carries it off with such an air - such a self-possession and easy grace! You cannot disturb the dead level of his self-esteem. To have him intruding at such a time, was more than I could bear. It completely unsettled me. Of course, when Miss Loring appeared, I was constrained, cold, embarrassed, distant - everything that was repulsive; while Dexter was as bland as a June morning - full of graceful compliments - attractive - winning. When I attempted some frozen speech, I could see a change in Miss Loring's manner, as if she had suddenly approached an iceberg; but, as often, Dexter would melt the ice away by one of his sunny smiles, and her face would grow radiant again."

"You exaggerate," said Mrs. Denison.

"The case admits of no exaggeration. I was too keenly alive to my own position; and saw only what was."

"The medium was distorted. Excited feelings are the eyes' magnifying glasses."

"It may be so." There was a modification in Hendrickson's manner. "I was excited. How could I help being so?"

"There existed no cause for it, Paul. Mr. Dexter had an equal right with yourself to visit Miss Loring."

"True."

"And an equal right to choose his own time."

"I will not deny it."

"Therefore, there was no reason in the abstract, why his complimentary call upon the lady should create in your mind unpleasant feelings towards the man. You had no more right to complain of his presence there, than he had to complain of yours."

"I confess it."

"There is one thing," pursued Mrs. Denison, "in which you disappoint me, Paul. You seem to lack a manly confidence in yourself. You are as good as Leon Dexter - aye, a better, truer man in every sense of the word - a man to please a woman at all worth pleasing, far better than he. And yet you permit him to elbow you aside, as it were, and to thrust you into a false position, if not into obscurity. If Miss Loring is the woman God has created for you, in the name of all that is holy, do not let another man usurp your rights. Do not let one like Dexter bear her off to gild a heartless home. Remember that Jessie is young, inexperienced, and unskilled in the ways of the world.

She is not schooled in the lore of love; cannot understand all its signs; and, above all, can no more look into your heart, than you can look into hers. How is she to know that you love her, if you stand coldly - I might say cynically - observant at a far distance. Paul! Paul! Women are not won in this way, as many a man has found to his sorrow, and as you will find in the present case, unless you act with more self-confidence and decision. Go to Miss Loring then, and show her, by signs not to be mistaken, that she has found favor in your eyes. Give her a chance to show you what her real feelings are; and my word for it, you will not find her as indifferent as you fear. If you gain any encouragement, make farther advances; and let her comprehend fully that you are an admirer. She will not play you false. Don't fear for a moment. She is above guile."

Mrs. Denison ceased. Her words had inspired Hendrickson with new feelings.

"As I parted from her to-day," he remarked, "she said, 'I shall be pleased to see you again.' I I felt that there was meaning in the words beyond a graceful speech. 'Not if I show myself as stupid as I have been this morning,' was my answer. Very quickly, and with some earnestness, she returned: 'I have never thought you stupid, Mr. Hendrickson.'"

"Well? And what then? Did you compliment her in return; or say something to fill her ears with music and make her heart tremble? You could have asked no better opportunity for giving the parting word that lingers longest and is oftenest conned over. What did you say to that, Paul?"

"I blundered out some meaningless things, and left her abruptly," said Hendrickson, with an impatient sweep of his hand. "I felt that her eyes were upon me, but had not the courage to lift my own and read their revelation."

"Too bad! Too bad! The old adage is true always - 'Faint heart never won fair lady' - and if you are not a little braver at heart, my young friend, you will lose this fair lady, whose hand may be had for the asking. So, I pray you, be warned in time. Go to her this very evening. You will probably find her alone. Dexter will hardly call twice in the same day; so you will be free from his intrusion. Let her see by tone, look, manner, word, that she has charmed your fancy. Show yourself an admirer. Then act as the signs indicate."

"I will," replied Hendrickson, speaking with enthusiasm.

"Go and heaven speed you! I have no fear as to the issue. But, Paul, let me warn you to repress your too sensitive feelings. Your conduct, heretofore, has not been such as to give Miss Loring any opportunity to judge of your real sentiments towards her. Your manner has been distant or constrained. She does not, therefore, understand you; and if her heart is really interested, she will be under constraint when she meets you to-night. Don't mind this. Be open, frank, at ease yourself. Keep your thoughts clear, and let not a pulse beat quicker than now."

"That last injunction goes too far, my good friend; for my heart gives a bound the moment my eyes rest upon her. So you see that mine is a desperate case."

"The more need of skill and coolness. A blunder may prove fatal."

Mr. Hendrickson rose, saying,

"Time passes. A good work were well done quickly. I will not linger when minutes are so precious."

"God speed you!" whispered Mrs. Denison, as they parted, a few minutes later at the door.

CHAPTER VI

IT was an hour from the time Mr. Hendrickson left the house of Mrs. Denison before he found himself in one of Mrs. Loring's parlors. He had been home, where a caller detained him.

Full ten minutes elapsed after his entrance, ere Jessie's light tread was heard on the stairs. She came down slowly, and as she entered the room, Hendrickson was struck with the singular expression of her face. At the first glance he scarcely recognized her.

"Are you not well, Miss Loring?" he asked, stepping forward to meet her.

His manner was warm, and his tones full of sympathy.

She smiled faintly as she answered -

"Not very well. I have a blinding headache."

Still holding the hand she had extended to him in meeting, Mr. Hendrickson led her to a sofa, and sat down by her side. He would have retained the hand, but she gently withdrew it, though not in a way that involved repulsion.

"I am sorry for your indisposition," he said, in a tone of interest so unusual for him, that Miss Loring lifted her eyes, which had fallen to the carpet, and looked at him half shyly -

T.S. Arthur

half interrogatingly.

"If you had sent me word that you were not well, Miss Loring" -

He paused, gazing very earnestly upon her face, into which crimsoning blushes began to come.

"I am pleased to meet you, Mr. Hendrickson. I did not wish to be excused," she answered, and then, as if she had been led to utter more than maidenly modesty approved, averted her face suddenly, and seemed confused. There followed a moment or two of silence; when her visitor said, leaning close to her, and speaking in a low, penetrating, steady voice -

"Your reply, Miss Loring, is an admission of more than I had expected - not more than I had hoped."

He saw her start, as if she had touched an electric wire. But her face remained averted.

"Miss Loring" -

Warmer words were on his lips, hut he hesitated to give them utterance. There was a pause. Motionless sat the young maiden, her face still partly turned away. Suddenly, and with an almost wild impulse, Hendrickson caught her hand, and raising it to his lips, said -

"I cannot hold back the words a moment longer, dear Miss Loring! From the hour I first looked into your face, I felt that we were made for each other; and now" -

But ere he could finish the sentence, Jessie had flung his hand away and started to her feet.

"Miss Loring!"

He was on his feet also. For some moments they stood gazing

at each other. The countenance of Miss Loring was of an ashen hue; her lips, almost as pallid as her cheeks, stood arching apart, and her eyes had the stare of one frightened by some fearful apparition.

"Miss Loring! pardon my folly! Your language made me bold to utter what had else slept in my heart eternally silent. Forget this hour!"

"Never! Never!" and she struck her hands together wildly. Her voice had in it a wail of suffering that sent a thrill to the heart of Paul Hendrickson.

Then recollecting herself, she struggled for the mastery over her feelings. He saw the struggle, and awaited the result. A brief interval sufficed to restore a degree of self-possession.

"I have nothing then to hope?" said the young man. His tones were evenly balanced.

"Too late! Too late!" she answered, in a hoarse voice. "The cup is dashed to pieces at my feet, and the precious wine spilled!"

"Oh, speak not thus! Recall the words!" exclaimed Hendrickson, reaching out his hands towards her.

But she moved back a pace or (sic) too repeating the sentence -

"Too late! Too late!"

"It is never too late!" urged the now almost desperate lover, advancing towards the maiden.

But retreating from him she answered in a warning voice -

"Touch me not! I am already pledged to another!"

"Impossible! Oh, light of my life!"

T.S. Arthur

"Sir! tempt me not!" she said interrupting him, "I have said it was too late! And now leave me. Go seek another to walk beside you in life's pleasant ways. Our paths diverge here."

"I will not believe it, Miss Loring! This is only a terrible dream!" exclaimed Hendrickson.

"A dream?" Jessie seemed clutching at the garments of some departing hope. "A dream!" She glanced around in a bewildered manner. "No - no - no." Almost despairingly the words came from her lips. "It is no dream, Paul Hendrickson! but a stern reality. And now," speaking quickly and with energy, "in Heaven's name leave me!"

"Not yet - not yet," said the young man, reaching for his hands and trying to take one of hers; but she put both of her hands behind her and stepped back several paces.

"Spare me the pain of a harsh word, Mr. Hendrickson. I have said - leave me!"

Her voice had acquired firmness.

"Oh, no! Smite me not with an unkind word," said Hendrickson. "I would not have that added to the heavy burden I seem doomed to bear. But ere I go, I would fain have more light, even if it should make the surrounding darkness black as pall."

His impassioned manner was gone.

"I am calm," he added, "calm as you are now, Miss Loring. The billows have fallen to the level plain under the pressure of this sudden storm. You have told me it was _too late_. You have said, 'leave me!' I believe you, and I will go. But, may I ask one question?"

"Speak, Mr. Hendrickson; but beware how you speak."

"Had I spoken as now this morning, would you have answered: 'Too late?'"

He was looking intently upon her face. She did not reply immediately, but seemed pondering. Hendrickson repeated the question.

"I have said that it was _now_ too late." Miss Loring raised her eyes and looked steadily upon him. "Go sir, and let this hour and this interview pass from your memory. If you are wise, you will forget it. Be just to me, sir. If I have betrayed the existence of any feeling towards you warmer than respect, it has been under sudden and strong temptation. As a man of honor, you must keep the secret inviolate."

There was not a sign of girlish weakness about the calm speaker. Her small head was erect; her slight body drawn to its full height; her measured tones betrayed not a ripple of feeling.

"I am affianced, and know my duty," she added. "Know it, and will perform it to the letter. And now, sir, spare me from this moment. And when we meet again, as meet no doubt we shall, let it be as friends - no more."

The pressure of despair was on the heart of Paul Hendrickson. He was not able to rally himself. He could not retain the calm exterior a little while before assumed.

"We part, then," he said, speaking in a broken voice - "part - and, ever after, a great gulf must lie between us! I go at your bidding," and he moved towards the door. "Farewell, Miss Loring." He extended his hand; she took it, and they stood looking into each other's eyes.

"God bless you, and keep you spotless as the angels!" he added, suddenly raising her hand to his lips, and kissing it with wild fervor. In the next moment the bewildered girl was alone.

CHAPTER VII

THE visit of Hendrickson was an hour too late, Dexter had already been there, and pressed his suit to a formal issue. The bold suitor had carried off the prize, while the timid one yet hesitated. Jessie went back to her room, after her interview with Paul Hendrickson, in spiritual stature no longer a half developed girl, but a full woman grown. The girl's strength would no longer have sustained her. Only the woman's soul, strong in principle and strong to endure, could bear up now. And the woman's soul shuddered in the conflict of passions that came like furies to destroy her - shuddered and bent, and writhed like some strong forest-tree in the maddening whirl of a tempest. But there was no faltering of purpose. She had passed her word - had made a solemn life-compact, and, she resolved to die, but not to waver.

The question as to whether she were right or wrong, it is not for us here to decide. We but record the fact. Few women after such a discovery would have ventured to move on a step farther. But Jessie was not an ordinary woman. She possessed a high sense of personal honor; and looked upon any pledge as a sacred obligation. Having consented to become the wife of Leon Dexter, she saw but one right course, and that was to perform, as best she could, her part of the contract.

How envied she was! Many wondered that Dexter should have turned aside for a portionless girl, when he might have led a jewelled bride to the altar. But though superficial, he had taste and discrimination enough to see that Jessie Loring was superior to all the maidens whom it had been his fortune to meet. And so, without pausing to look deeply into her heart, or take note of its peculiar aspirations and impulses, he boldly pressed forward resolved to win. And he did win; and in winning, thought, like many another foolish man, that to win the loveliest, was to secure the highest happiness. Fatal error! Doubly fatal!

It is impossible for any woman to pass through an ordeal like the one that was testing the quality of Jessie Loring, and not show signs of the inward strife. It is in no way surprising, therefore, that, in her exterior, a marked change soon became visible. There was a certain dignity and reserve, verging, at times, on coldness, not seen prior to her (sic) engagement - and a quiet suppression of familiarity, even with her most intimate friends. The same marked change was visible in her intercourse with Mr. Dexter. She did not meet him with that kind of repulsion which is equivalent to pushing back with the hand. She accepted his loving ardor of speech and act; but passively. There was no responsive warmth.

At first Mr. Dexter was puzzled, and his ardent feelings chilled. He loved, admired, almost worshipped the beautiful girl from whom consent had been extorted, and her quiet, cold manner, troubled his sorely. Glimpses of the real truth dawned into his mind. He let his thoughts go back, and went over again, in retrospection, every particular of their intercourse - dwelling minutely upon her words, looks, manner and emotions at the time he first pressed his suit upon her. The result was far from satisfactory. She had not met his advances as he had hoped; but rather fled from him - and he had gained her only by pursuit. Her ascent had not come warmly from her heart, but burdened with a sigh. Mr. Dexter felt that though she was his, she had not been fairly won. The conviction troubled him.

"I will release her," he said, in a sudden glow of generous enthusiasm. But Mr. Dexter had not the nobility for such a step. He was too selfish a man to relinquish the prize.

"I will woo and win her still." This was to him a more satisfactory conclusion. But he had won all of her in his power to gain. Her heart was to him a sealed book. He could not unclasp the volume, nor read a single page.

Earnestly at times did Jessie strive to appear attractive in the eyes of her betrothed - to meet his ardor with returning warmth. But the effort was accompanied with so much pain, that suffering was unable to withdraw wholly beneath a veil of smiles.

The wordy, restless pleasure evinced by Mrs. Loring, was particularly annoying to Jessie; so much so that any allusion by her aunt to the approaching marriage, was almost certain to cloud her brow. And yet so gratified was this worldly-minded woman, at the good fortune of her niece in securing so (sic) brillant an alliance, that it seemed as if, for a time, she could talk of nothing else.

Mr. Dexter urged an early marriage, while Jessie named a period nearly a year in advance; but, as she could give no valid reason for delaying their happiness so long, the time was shortened to four months. As the day approached, the pressure on the heart of Miss Loring grew heavier.

"Oh, if I could die!" How many times in the silence of night and in the loneliness of her chamber did her lips give forth this utterance.

But the striving spirit could not lay down its burden thus.

Not once, since the exciting interview we have described, had Paul and Jessie met. At places of fashionable amusement she was a constant attendant in company with Dexter, who was proud of her beauty. But though her eyes searched everywhere in the crowded audiences, in no instance did she recognize the face of Hendrickson. In festive companies, where he had been a constant attendant, she missed his presence. Often she heard him inquired after, yet only once did the answer convey any intelligence. It was at an evening party. "Where is Mr. Hendrickson? It is a long time since I have seen him," she heard a lady say. Partly turning she recognized Mrs. Denison as the person addressed. The answer was in so low a tone that her ear did not make it out, though she listened with suspended breath.

"Ah! I'm sorry," responded the other. "What is the cause?"

"A matter of the heart, I believe," said Mrs. Denison.

"Indeed is he very much depressed?"

"He is changed," was the simple reply.

"Who was the lady?"

Jessie did not hear the answer.

"You don't tell me so!" In a tone of surprise, and the lady glanced around the room.

"And he took it very much to heart?" she went on.

"Yes. I think it will change the complexion of his whole life," said Mrs. Denison. "He is a man of deep feeling - somewhat peculiar; over diffident; and not given to showing himself off to the best advantage. But he is every inch a man - all gold and no tinsel! I have known him from boyhood, and speak of his quality from certain knowledge."

"He will get over it," remarked the lady. "Men are not apt to go crazy after pretty girls. The market is full of such attractions."

"It takes more than a painted butterfly to dazzle him, my friend," said Mrs. Denison. "His eyes are too keen, and go below the surface at a glance. The woman he loves may regard the fact as a high testimonial."

"But you don't suppose he is going to break his heart over this matter."

"No - oh, no! That is an extreme disaster."

"He will forget her in time; and there are good fish in the sea yet."

"Time is the great restorer," said Mrs. Denison; "and time will show, I trust, that good will come from this severe trial which my young friend is now enduring. These better natures are oftenest exposed to furnace heat, for only they have gold enough to stand the ordeal of fire."

"He is wrong to shut himself out from society."

"So I tell him. But he says 'wait - wait, I am not strong enough yet.'"

"He must, indeed, take the matter deeply to heart."

"He does."

Here the voice fell to such a low measure, that Jessie lost all distinction of words. But the few sentences which had reached her ears disturbed her spirit profoundly - too profoundly to make even a ripple on the surface. No one saw a change on her countenance, and her voice, answering a moment after to the voice of a friend, betrayed no unusual sign of feeling.

And this was all she had heard of him for months.

Once, a little while before her marriage, she met him. It was a few weeks after these brief unsatisfactory sentences had troubled the waters of her spirit. She had been out with her aunt for the purpose of selecting her wedding attire; and after a visit to the dressmaker's, was returning alone, her aunt wishing to make a few calls at places where Jessie did not care to go. She was crossing one of the public squares when the thought of Hendrickson came suddenly into her mind. Her eyes were cast down at the moment. Looking up, involuntarily, she paused, for within a few paces was the young man himself, approaching from the opposite direction. He paused also, and they stood with eyes riveted upon each other's faces - both, for a time, too much embarrassed to speak. Their hands had mutually clasped, and Hendrickson was holding that of Jessie tightly compressed within his own.

The first to regain self-possession was Miss Loring. With a quick motion she withdrew her hand, and moved back a single step. The mantling flush left her brow, and the startled eyes looked calmly into the young man's face.

"Have you been away from the city, Mr. Hendrickson?" she inquired, in a voice that gave but few signs of feeling.

"No." He could not trust himself to utter more than a single word.

"I have missed you from the old places," she said.

"Have you? It is something, even to be missed?" He could not suppress the tremor in his voice.

"Good morning!"

Jessie almost sprang past him, and hurried away. The tempter was at her side; and she felt it to be an hour of weakness. She must either yield or fly - and she fled; fled with rapid unsteady feet, pausing not until the door of her own chamber shut out all the world and left her alone with Heaven. Weak, trembling, exhausted she bowed herself, and in anguish of spirit prayed -

"Oh, my Father, sustain me! Give me light, strength, patience, endurance. I am walking darkly, and the way is rough and steep. Let me not fall. The floods roar about me - let me not sink beneath them. My heart is failing under its heavy burden. Oh, bear me up! The sky is black - show me some rift in the

T.S. Arthur

clouds, for I am fainting in this rayless night. And oh, if I dare pray for *him* - if the desire for his happiness springs from no wrong sentiment - let this petition find favor - as he asked that I might be kept spotless as the angels, so keep him; and after he has passed through the furnace, let not even the smell of fire be upon him. Send him a higher blessing than that which he has lost. Oh Lord, give strength to both - especially to her whose voice is now ascending, for she is weakest, and will have most to endure."

For a long time after the murmur of prayer had died on her lips, Jessie remained prostrate. When she arose at last, it was with a slow, weary movement, dreary eyes, and absent manner. The shock of this meeting had been severe - disturbing her too profoundly for even the soothing influence of prayer. She did not arise from her knees comforted - scarcely strengthened. A kind of benumbing stupor followed.

"What ails the girl!" said Mrs. Loring to herself as she vainly strove at dinner-time to draw her forth into lively conversation. "She gets into the strangest states - just like her poor mother! And like her I'm afraid, sometimes, will make herself and every one else around her miserable. I pity Leon Dexter, if this be so. He may find that his caged bird will not sing. Already the notes are few and far between; and little of the old sweetness remains."

CHAPTER VIII

A FEW days after the meeting between Mr. Hendrickson and Miss Loring, as just mentioned, Mr. Dexter received the following communication:

"DEAR SIR - I am scarcely well enough acquainted with you to venture this note and request; but I happen to know of something so vital to your happiness, that I cannot feel conscience-clear and not ask an interview. I shall be at home this evening.

"ALICE DENISON."

Early in the evening, Dexter was at the house of Mrs. Denison.

"You have frightened me my dear madam!" he said, almost abruptly, as he entered the parlor, where he found her awaiting him.

"I have presumed on a slight acquaintance, Mr. Dexter, to ask an interview on a very delicate subject," Mrs. Denison replied. "May I speak freely, and without danger of offending, when no offence is designed?"

"I have not had the pleasure of knowing you intimately, Mrs. Denison," replied the visitor, "but it has been no fault of mine. I have always held you in high regard; and always been gratified with our passing intercourse on the few occasions it has been my privilege to meet you. That you have felt enough concern for my welfare to ask this interview, gratifies me. Say on - and speak freely. I am eager to hear."

"You are about to marry Jessie Loring," said Mrs. Denison.

"I am." And Dexter fixed his eyes with a look of earnest inquiry upon the lady's face.

Mrs. Denison had come to the subject more abruptly than she at first intended, and she was already in doubt as to her next remark; but there could be no holding back now.

"Are you sure, Mr. Dexter, that you possess her undivided heart?"

"I marvel at your question, madam!" he answered, with a start, and in a tone of surprise.

"Calmly, my friend." And Mrs. Denison, who was a woman of remarkably clear perceptions, laid her hand upon his arm. "I am not questioning idly, nor to serve any sinister or hidden purpose - but am influenced by higher motives. Nor am I acting at the instance of another. What passes between us this evening shall be sacred. I said that I knew of something vital to your happiness; therefore I asked this interview. And now ponder well my question, and be certain that you get the right answer."

Dexter let his eyes fall. He sat for a long while silent, but evidently in earnest thought.

"Have you her full, free, glad assent to the approaching union?" asked Mrs. Denison, breaking in upon his silence. She saw a shade of impatience on his countenance as he looked up and checked the words that were on his lips, by saying:

"Marriage is no light thing, my young friend. It is a relation which, more than any other, makes or mars the future; and when entered into, should be regarded as the must solemn act of life. Here all error is fatal. The step once taken, it cannot be retraced. Whether the path be rough or even, it must be pursued to the end. If the union be harmonious - internally so, I mean - peace, joy, interior delight will go on, finding daily increase - if inharmonious, eternal discord will curse the married partners. Do not be angry with me then, for pressing the question - Have you her full, free, glad, assent to the approaching union? If not, pause - for your love-freighted bark may be drifting fast upon the breakers - and not yours only, but hers.

"I have reason to fear, Mr. Dexter," continued Mrs. Denison, seeing that her visitor did not attempt to reply, but sat looking at her in a kind of bewildered surprise, "that you pressed your suit too eagerly, and gained a half unwilling consent. Now, if this be so, you are in great danger of making shipwreck. An ordinary woman - worldly, superficial, half-hearted, or no-hearted - even if she did not really love you, would find ample compensation in your fortune, and in the social advantages it must secure. But depend upon it, sir, these will not fill the aching void that must be in Jessie Loring's heart, if you have no power to fill it with your image - for she is no ordinary woman. I have observed her carefully since this engagement, and grieve to see that she is not happy. Have you seen no change?"

Mrs. Denison waited for an answer.

"She is not so cheerful; I have noticed that," replied the young man.

"Have you ever questioned in your own mind as to the cause?"

"Often."

"And what was the solution!"

"I remain ignorant of the cause."

"Mr. Dexter; *I* am not ignorant of the cause!"

"Speak, then, in Heaven's name!"

The young man betrayed a deeper excitement than he wished to manifest. He had been struggling with himself.

"Her heart is not yours!" said Mrs. Denison, with suppressed feeling. "It is a hard saying, but I speak it in the hope of saving both you and the maiden from a life of wretchedness."

"By what authority and under what instigation do you say this?" was demanded almost angrily. "You are going a step too far, madam!"

The change in his manner was very sudden.

"I speak from myself only," replied Mrs. Denison, calmly.

"If her heart is not mine, whose is it?" Dexter showed strong excitement.

"I am not her confidant."

"Who is? Somebody must speak from her, if I am to credit your assertion."

"Calm yourself, my young friend," said Mrs. Denison; "there are signs which a woman can read as plainly as if they were written words; and I have felt too deep an interest in this matter not to have marked every sign. Miss Loring is not happy, and the shadow upon her spirit grows darker every day. Before this engagement, her glad soul looked ever out in beauty from her eyes; now - but I need not describe to you the change. You have noted its progress. It is an extreme conclusion that her heart is not in the alliance she is about to form."

A long silence followed.

"If you were certain that I am right - if, with her own lips, Jessie Loring were to confirm what I have said - what then?"

"I would release her from this engagement; and she might go her ways! The world is wide."

He spoke with some bitterness.

"The way is plain, then. From what I have said, you are fully warranted in talking to her without reserve. Quote me if you please. Say that I made bold to assert that you did not possess the key that would unlock the sacred places of her heart; and you may add further, that I say the *key is held by another*. This will bring the right issue. If she truly loves you, there will be no mistaking her response. If she accepts the release you offer, happy will you be in making the most fortunate escape of your life."

"I will do it!" exclaimed Dexter, rising, "and this very night!"

"If done at all, it were well done quickly," said Mrs. Denison, rising also. "And now, my young friend, let what will be the result, think of me as one who, under the pressure of a high sense of responsibility, has simply discharged a painful duty. I have no personal or private ends to gain; all I desire is to save two hearts from making shipwreck. If successful, I shall have my reward."

"One question, Mrs. Denison," said Dexter, as they were about separating. "Its answer may give me light, and the strength to go forward. I have marked your words and manner very closely; and this is my conclusion: You not only believe that I do not possess the love of Jessie Loring, but your thought points to another man whom you believe does rule in her affections. Am I wrong?"

The suddenness of the question confused Mrs. Denison. Her eyes sunk under his gaze, and for some moments her self possession was lost. But, rallying herself, she answered:

"Not wholly wrong."

Dexter's countenance grew dark.

"His name! - give me his name!"

He spoke with agitation.

"That is going a step too far," said Mrs. Denison, with firmness.

"Is it Hendrickson?"

Dexter looked keenly into the lady's face.

"A step too far, sir," she repeated. "I cannot answer your inquiry."

"You *must* answer it, madam!" He was imperative. "I demand the yes or no. Is it or is it not Paul Hendrickson?"

"Your calmer reason, sir, will tell you to-morrow that I was right in refusing to give any man's name in this connection," replied Mrs. Denison. "I am pained to see you so much disturbed. My hope was, that you would go to Miss Loring in the grave dignity of manhood - But, while in this spirit of angry excitement, I pray you keep far from her."

"Hendrickson is the man!" said Dexter, his brows still contracting heavily. "But if he still hopes to rival me in Jessie's love, he will find himself vastly in error. No, no, madam! If it is for him you are interested, you had better give it up. I passed him in the race long ago!"

A feeling of disgust arose in the mind of Mrs. Denison, mingled with a stronger feeling of contempt. But she answered without a visible sign of either.

"I am sorry that you have let the form of any person come in to give right thought and honorable purpose a distorting bias. I did hope that you would see Miss Loring under the influence of a better state. And I pray you still to be calm, rational, generous, manly. Go to her in a noble, unselfish spirit. If you love her truly you desire her happiness; and to make her happy, would even release her pledged hand, were such a sacrifice needed."

"You give me credit for more virtue than I claim to possess," was answered, a little sarcastically. "Love desires to hold, not lose its object."

"Enough, my young friend," said Mrs. Denison, in her calm, earnest way. "We will not bandy words - that would be fruitless. I grieve that you should have misunderstood me in even the least thing, or let the slightest suggestion of a sinister motive find a lodgment in your mind. I have had no purpose but a good one to serve, and shall be conscience-clear in the matter. A more delicate task than this was never undertaken. That I have not succeeded according to my wishes, is no matter of surprise."

"Good evening, madam!"

Dexter bowed with a cold formality.

"Good evening!" was mildly returned.

And so the young man went away.

"I fear that only harm will come of this," said Mrs. Denison, as she retired from the door. "I meant it for the best, and pray that no evil may follow the indiscretion, if such it be!"

CHAPTER IX

MRS. DENISON'S fears were prophetic. Evil, not good, came of her well meant efforts to prevent the coming sacrifice. Instead of awakening generous impulses in the mind of Leon Dexter, only anger and jealousy were aroused; and as they gained strength, love withdrew itself, for love could not breathe the same atmosphere. The belief that Hendrickson was the man to whom Mrs. Denison referred, was fully confirmed by this fact. Dexter had resolved to see Miss Loring that very evening, and was only a short distance from her home, and in sight of the door, when he saw a man ascend the steps and ring. He stopped and waited. A servant came to the door and the caller entered. For a time, the question was revolved as to whether he should follow, or not.

"It is Hendrickson. I'll wager my life on it!" - he muttered, grinding his teeth together. "There is a cursed plot on foot, and this insinuating, saintly Mrs. Denison, is one of the plotters! My very blood is seething at the thought. Shall I go in now, and confront him at his devilish work?"

"It were better not," he said, after a brief struggle with his feelings. "I am too excited, and cannot answer for myself. A false step now might ruin all. First, let me cage my singing bird, and then" -

He strode onwards and passed the house of Mrs. Loring with rapid steps. There was a light in the parlor, and he heard the sound of voices. Ten minutes after, he returned - the light was there still; but though he went by slowly, with noiseless footsteps - listening - not a murmur reached his ears.

"He is there, a subtle tempter, whispering his honeyed allurements!" It was the fiend Jealousy speaking in his heart. "Madness!" he ejaculated, and he strode up the marble steps. Grasping the bell, he resolved to enter. But something held back his hand, and another voice said - "Wait! Wait! A single error now were fatal."

Slowly he descended, his ear bent to the windows, listening - slowly, still listening, he moved onwards again; his whole being convulsed in a stronger conflict of passion than he had ever known - reason at fault and perception blindfold.

A full half hour had elapsed, when Dexter reappeared. He was in a calmer frame of mind. Reason was less at fault, and perception clearer. His purpose was to go in now, confront Jessie and Mr. Hendrickson, and act from that point onward as the nature of the case might suggest. He glanced at the parlor windows. There was no light there now. The visitor had departed. He felt relieved, yet disappointed.

"Is Miss Loring at home?" he asked of the servant.

"Yes, sir." And he entered. The lights, which were burning low in the parlors, were raised, and Dexter sat down and awaited the appearance of Jessie.

How should he meet her? With the warmth of a lover, or the distance of a mere acquaintance? Would it be wise to speak of his interview with Mrs. Denison, or let that subject pass untouched by even the remotest allusion? Mr. Dexter was still in debate, when he heard some one descending the stairs. Steps were in the passage near the door. He arose, and stood expectant.

"Miss Loring says, will you please excuse her this evening?"

"Excuse her!" Mr. Dexter could not veil his surprise. "Why does she wish to be excused, Mary?"

"I don't know sir. She didn't say."

"Is she sick?"

"I don't think she is very well. Something isn't right with her, poor child!"

"What isn't right with her?"

"I don't know, sir. But she was crying when I went into her room."

"Crying?"

"Yes, sir; and she cries a great deal, all alone there by herself, sir," added Mary, who had her own reasons for believing that Dexter was not really the heart-choice of Jessie - and with the tact of her sex, took it upon herself to throw a little cold water over his ardor. It may be that she hoped to give it a thorough chill.

"What does she cry about, Mary?"

"Dear knows, sir! I often wonder to see it, and she so soon to be married. It doesn't look just natural. There's something wrong."

"Wrong? How wrong, Mary?"

"That's just what I asked myself over and over again," replied the girl.

"She had a visitor here to-night," said Dexter, after a moment or two. He tried to speak indifferently; but the quick perception of Mary detected the covert interest in his tones.

"Yes." A single cold (sic) monosylable was her reply.

"Who was he?"

"'Deed I don't know, sir."

"Was he a stranger?"

"I didn't see him, sir," answered Mary.

"You let him in?"

"No, sir. The cook went to the door."

Dexter bit his lips with disappointment.

"Will you say to Miss Loring that I wish to see her particularly to-night."

Mary hesitated.

"Why don't you take up my request?" He spoke with covert impatience.

"I am sure she wishes to be excused to-night," persisted the girl. "She's not at all herself; and it will be cruel to drag her down."

But Dexter waved his hand, and said, sharply:

"I wish to hear no more from you, Miss Pert! Go to Miss Loring, and tell her that she will confer a favor by seeing me this evening. I can receive no apology but sickness."

Jessie was sitting as Mary had left her, both hands covering her face, when that kind-hearted creature returned.

"It's too much!" exclaimed the girl, as she entered. "He must see you, he says. I told him you wasn't well, and wished to be excused. But no, he must see you! Something's gone wrong with him. He's all out of sorts, and spoke as if he'd take my head off. He really frightened me!"

Jessie drew a long deep sigh.

"If I must, I must," she said, rising and looking at her face in the mirror.

"*I* wouldn't go one step, Miss Jessie, if I were you. I'd like to see the man who dared order me down in this style. He's jealous; that's the long and short of it. Punish him - he deserves it."

"Jealous, Mary?" Miss Loring turned to the girl with a startled look. "Why do you say that?"

"Oh, he asked me if you hadn't a visitor to-night."

"Well?"

"I said yes. Only 'yes,' and no more."

"Why yes, and no more?" asked Miss Loring.

"D'ye think I was going to gratify him! What business had he to ask whether you had a visitor or not? You ain't sold to him."

"Mary!" There was reproof in the look and voice of Miss Loring. "You must not speak so of Mr. Dexter."

"Well, I won't if it displeases you. But I was downright mad with him."

"You said yes to his question. What then, Mary?"

"Oh, then he wanted to know who he was."

"Did you tell him?"

"No."

"Why? And what did you answer?"

"I wasn't going to gratify him; and I said that I didn't know."

"Well?"

"'Was he a stranger?' said he. 'I didn't see him,' said I. 'You let him in?' said he. 'No, the cook went to the door,' said I. You should have seen him then. He was baffled. Then looking almost savage, he bid me tell you that you must see him to-night."

"*Must* see him! Did he say *must*?"

There was rebellion in Jessie's voice.

"Well no, not just that word. But he looked and meant it, which is all the same."

"Then he doesn't know who called to see me?"

"Not from all he got from me, miss. But you're not going down?"

"Yes, Mary; I will see him as he desires. Go and say that I will join him in a few minutes."

The girl obeyed, and Jessie, after struggling a few moments with her feelings, went down to the parlor, where Mr. Dexter awaited her.

"I am sorry to learn that you are not well this evening," said the young man, as he advanced across the room, with his eyes fixed intently on the face of his betrothed. She tried to smile, and receive him with her usual kindness of manner. But this was impossible. She been profoundly disturbed, and that too recently for self-possession.

"What ails you? Has anything happened?"

Jessie had not yet trusted her lips with words. The tones of Dexter evinced some fretfulness.

"I am not very well," she said, partly turning away her face that she might avoid the searching scrutiny of his eyes.

Dexter took her hand and led her to a sofa. They sat down, side by side, in silence - ice between them.

"Have you been indisposed all day?" inquired Dexter.

"I have not been very well for some time," was answered in a husky voice, and in a manner that he thought evasive.

Again there was silence.

"I called to see Mrs. Denison this evening," said Dexter; and then waited almost breathlessly for a response, looking at Jessie stealthily to note the effect of his words.

"Did you?"

There was scarcely a sign of interest in her voice.

"Yes. You have met her, I believe?"

"A few times."

"Have you seen her recently?"

"No."

Dexter gained nothing by this advance.

"What do you think of her?" he added, after a pause.

"She is a lady of fine social qualities and superior worth."

Again the young man was silent. He could not discover by Jessie's manner that she had any special interest in Mrs. Denison. This was some relief; for it removed the impression that there was an understanding between them.

"I don't admire her a great deal," he said, with an air of indifference. "She's a little too prying and curious; and I'm afraid, likes to gossip."

"Ah! I thought her particularly free from that vice."

"I had that impression also. But my interview this evening gave me a different estimate of her character."

"Did you come from Mrs. Denison's directly here?" asked Jessie in a changed tone, as if some thought of more than common interest had flitted through her mind. This change Dexter did not fail to observe.

"I did," was his answer.

"Then I may infer," said Jessie, "that your pressing desire to see me this evening has grown out of something you heard from the lips of Mrs. Denison. Am I right in this conclusion?"

Dexter was not quite prepared for this. After a slight hesitation he answered -

"Partly so."

The cold indifferent manner of Jessie Loring passed away directly.

"If you have anything to communicate, as of course you have, say on, Mr. Dexter."

As little prepared was he for this; and quite as little for the almost stately air with which Jessie drew up her slight form, returning his glances with so steady a gaze that his eyes fell.

The hour and the opportunity had come. But Leon Dexter had neither the manliness nor the courage to speak.

"Did Mrs. Denison introduce my name?" asked Jessie, seeing that her lover had failed to answer. There was not a quiver in her voice, nor the slightest failing in her eyes.

"Yes; casually." Dexter spoke with evasion.

"What did she say?"

"Nothing but what was good," said Dexter, now trying to resume his wonted pleasant exterior. "What else could she say? You look as if there had been a case of slander."

"She said something in connection with my name," answered Jessie firmly, "that disturbed you. Now as you have disclosed so much, I must know all."

"I have made no disclosures." Dexter seemed annoyed.

"You said you were at Mrs. Denison's."

"Yes."

"And said it with a meaning. I noticed both tone and manner. You came directly here, according to your own admission, and asked for me. Not being well, I desired to be excused. But you would take no excuse. Your manner to the servant was not only disturbed, but imperative. To me it is constrained, and altogether different from anything I have hitherto noticed. So much is disclosed. Now I wish you to go on and tell the whole story. Then we shall understand each other. What has Mrs. Denison said about me that has so ruffled your feelings?"

There was no retreat for the perplexed young man. He must go forward in some path - straight or tortuous - manly or evasive. There was too much apparent risk in the former; and so he chose the latter. All at once his exterior changed. The clouded brow put on a sunny aspect.

"Forgive me, dear Jessie!" he said with ardor, and a restored tenderness of manner. "True love has ever a touch of jealousy; and something that Mrs. Denison intimated aroused that darker passion. But the shadowed hour has passed, and I am in the clear sunlight again."

He raised her hand to his lips, and kissed it with fervor.

"What did she intimate?" asked Miss Loring. Her manner was less excited, and her tone less imperative.

"What I now see to be false," said Dexter. "I was disturbed because I imagined intrigue, and a purpose to rob me of something I prize more dearly than life - the love of my Jessie."

"Intrigue!" was answered; "you fill me with surprise. Mrs. Denison, if I understand her, is incapable of anything so dishonorable."

"I don't know." Mr. Dexter spoke with the manner of one in doubt, and as if questioning his own thoughts. "She has filled my mind with dark suspicions. Why, Jessie!" and he assumed a more animated exterior, "she went so far as to intimate a disingenuous spirit in you!"

"In me!" Miss Loring's surprise was natural. "Disingenuousness!"

"That word is not the true one," said Dexter. "What she said meant something more."

"What?"

"That you were - but I will not pain your ears, darling! Forgive my foolish indignation. Love with me is so vital a thing, that the remotest suspicion of losing its object, brings smarting pain. You are all the world to me, Jessie, and the intimation" -

T.S. Arthur

"Of what, Leon?"

He had left the sentence unfinished. Dexter was holding one of her hands. She did not attempt to withdraw it.

"That you were false to me!"

The words caused Miss Loring to spring to her feet. Bright spots burned on her cheeks, and her eyes flashed.

"False to you! What did she mean by such words?" was demanded.

"It was the entering wedge of suspicion," said Dexter. "But the trick has failed. My heart tells me that you are the soul of honor. If I was disturbed, is that a cause of wonder? Would not such an allegation against me have disturbed you? It would! But that your heart is pure and true as an angel's, I best know of all the living. Dear Jessie!" and he laid a kiss upon her burning cheek,

"I shall never cease to blame myself for the part I have played this evening. Had I loved you less I had been calmer."

"False in what way?" asked Miss Loring, unsatisfied with so vague an answer.

"False to your vows, of course. What else could she mean?"

"Did she say that?"

"No - of course not. But she conveyed the meaning as clearly as if she had uttered the plainest language."

"What were her words?" asked Miss Loring.

"I cannot repeat them. She spoke with great caution, keeping remote, as to words, from the matter first in her thought, yet filling my mind with vague distrust, or firing it with jealousy at every sentence."

"Can you fix a single clear remark - something that I can repeat?"

"Not one. The whole interview impresses me like a dream. Only the disturbance remains. But let it pass as a dream, darling - a nightmare created by some spirit of evil. A single glance into your dear face and loving eyes rebukes my folly and accuses me of wrong. We are all the world to each other, and no shadow even shall come again between our souls and happiness."

Jessie resumed her seat and questioned no farther. Was she satisfied with the explanation? Of course not. But her lover was adroit, and she became passive.

"You cannot wonder now," he said, "that I was so anxious to see you this evening. I might have spared you this interview, and it would have been better, perhaps, if I had done so. But excited lovers are not always the most reasonable beings in the world. I could not have slept to-night. Now I shall find the sweetest slumber that has yet refreshed my spirit - and may your sleep, dearest, be gentle as the sleep of flowers! I will leave you now, for I remember that you are far from being well this evening. It will grieve me to think that my untimely intrusion, and this disturbing hour, may increase the pain you suffer or rob you of a moment's repose. - Good night, love!" and he kissed her tenderly. "Good night, precious one!" he added. "May angels be your companions through the dark watches, and bring you to a glorious morning!"

He left her, and moved towards the door; yet lingered, for his mind was not wholly at ease in regard to the state of Jessie's feelings. She had not repelled him in any way - but his ardent words and acts were too passively received. She was standing where he had parted from her, with her eyes upon the floor.

"Jessie!"

T.S. Arthur

She looked up.

"Good night, dear!"

"Good night, Mr. Dexter."

"Mr. Dexter!" The young man repeated the words between his teeth, as he passed into the street a moment afterwards. "Mr. Dexter! and in tones that were cold as an icicle!"

He strode away from the house of Mrs. Loring, but little comforted by his interview with Jessie, and with the fiend Jealousy a permanent guest in his heart.

CHAPTER X

LEON DEXTER was not wrong in his suspicions. It was Hendrickson who visited Miss Loring on the evening of his interview with Mrs. Denison. The young man had striven, with all the power he possessed, to overcome his fruitless passion - but striven in vain. - The image of Miss Loring had burned itself into his heart, and become ineffaceable. The impression she had made upon him was different from that made by any woman he had yet chanced to meet, and he felt that, in some mysterious way, their destinies were bound up together. That, in her heart, she preferred him to the man who was about to sacrifice her at the marriage altar he no longer doubted.

"Is it right to permit this sacrifice?" The question had thrust itself upon him for days and weeks.

"Leon Dexter cannot fill the desire of her heart." Thus he talked with himself. "She does not love; and to such a woman marriage unblessed by love must be a condition worse than death. No - no! It shall not be! Steadily she is moving on, nerved by a false sense of honor; and unless some one comes to the rescue, the fatal vow will be made that seals the doom of her happiness and mine. It must not - shall not be! Who so fitting as I to be her rescuer? She loves me! Eyes, lips, countenance, tones, gestures, all have been my witnesses. Only an hour too late! Too late? No - no! I will not believe the words! She shall yet be mine!"

It was in this spirit, and under the pressure of such feelings, that Paul Hendrickson visited Jessie Loring on the night Dexter saw him enter the house. The interview was not a very long one, as the reader knows. He sent up his card, and Miss Loring returned for answer, that she would see him in a few moments. Full five minutes elapsed before she left her room. It had taken her nearly all that time to school her agitated feelings; for on seeing his name, her heart had leaped with an irrepressible impulse. She looked down into her heart, and questioned as to the meaning of this disturbance. The response was clear. Paul Hendrickson was more to her than any living man!

"He should have spared me an interview, alone," she said to herself. "Better for both of us not to meet."

This was her state of feeling, when after repressing, as far as possible, every unruly emotion, she left her room and took her way down stairs.

"Is not this imprudent?" The mental question arrested the footsteps of Miss Loring, ere she had proceeded five paces from the door of her chamber.

"Is not what imprudent?" was answered back in her thoughts.

"What folly is this!" she said, in self-rebuke, and passed onward.

"Miss Loring!" There was too much feeling in Hendrickson's manner. But its repression, under the circumstances, was impossible.

"Mr. Hendrickson!" The voice of Miss Loring betrayed far more of inward disturbance than she wished to appear.

Their hands met. They looked into each other's eyes - then stood for some moments in mutual embarrassment.

"You are almost a stranger," said Jessie, conscious that any remark was better, under the circumstances, than silence.

"Am I?" Hendrickson still held her hand, and still gazed into her eyes. The ardor of his glances reminded her of duty and of danger. Her hand disengaged itself from his - her eyes fell to the floor - a deep crimson suffused her countenance. They seated themselves - she on the sofa, and he on a chair drawn close beside, or rather nearly in front of her. How heavily beat the maiden's heart! What a pressure, almost to suffocation, was on her bosom! She felt an impending sense of danger, but lacked the resolution to flee.

"Miss Loring," said Hendrickson, his unsteady voice betraying his inward agitation, "when I last saw you" -

"Sir!" There was a sudden sternness in the young girl's voice, and a glance of warning in her eye. But the visitor was not to be driven from his purpose.

"It is *not* too late, Jessie Loring!" He spoke with eagerness.

She made a motion as if about to rise, but he said in a tone that restrained her.

"No, Miss Loring! You *must* hear what I have to say to-night."

She grew very pale; but looked at him steadily.

So unexpected were his intimations - so imperative his manner, that she was, in a degree, bereft for the time of will.

"You should have spared me this, Mr. Hendrickson," she answered, sadly, and with a gentle rebuke in her tones.

"I would endure years of misery to save you from a moment's pain!" was quickly replied. "And it is in the hope of being able to call down Heaven's choicest blessings on your head, that I am here to-night. Let me speak without reserve. Will you

T.S. Arthur

hear me?"

Miss Loring made no sigh; only her eyelids drooped slowly, until the bright orbs beneath were hidden and the dark lashes lay softly on her colorless cheeks.

"There is one thing, Miss Loring," he began, "known to yourself and me alone. It is our secret. Nay! do not go! Let me say on now, and I will ever after hold my peace. If this marriage contract, so unwisely made, is not broken, two lives will be made wretched - yours and mine. You do not love Mr. Dexter! You cannot love him! That were as impossible as for light to be enamored of dark" -

"I will not hear you!" exclaimed Miss Loring, starting to her feet. But Hendrickson caught her hand and restrained her by force.

"You must hear me!" he answered passionately.

"I dare not!"

"This once! I must speak now, and you must hear! God has given you freedom of thought and freedom of will. Let both come into their true activity. The holiest things of your life demand this, Miss Loring. Sit down and be calm again, and let us talk calmly. I will repress all excitement, and speak with reason. You shall hearken and decide. There - I thank you" -

Jessie had resumed her seat.

"We have read each other's hearts, Miss Loring," Hendrickson went on. His voice had regained its firmness, and he spoke in low, deep, emphatic tones. "I, at least, have read yours, and you know mine. Against your own convictions and your own feelings, you have been coerced into an engagement of marriage with a man you do not, and never can, love as a wife should love a husband. Consummate that engagement, and years of wretchedness lie before you. I say nothing of Mr.

Dexter as regards honor, probity, and good feeling. I believe him to be a man of high integrity. His character before the world is blameless - his position one to be envied. But you do not love him - you cannot love him. Nay it is idle to repel the assertion. I have looked down too deeply into your heart. I know how its pulses beat, Jessie Loring! There is only one living man who has the power to unlock its treasures of affection. To all others it must remain eternally sealed. I speak solemnly - not vainly. And your soul echoes the truth of my words. It is not yet too late!"

"You should not have said this, Mr. Hendrickson!" Jessie resolutely disengaged the hand he had taken, and was clasping with almost vice-like pressure, and arose to her feet. He did not rise, but sat looking up into her pale suffering face, with the light of hope, which for a moment had flushed his own, fast decaying.

"You should not have said this, Mr. Hendrickson!" she repeated, in a steadier voice. "It is too late, and only makes my task the harder - my burden heavier. But God helping me, I will walk forward in the right path, though my feet be lacerated at every step."

"Is it a right path, Miss Loring? I declare it to be the wrong path!" said Hendrickson.

"Let God and my own conscience judge!" was firmly answered. "And now, sir, leave me. Oh, leave me."

"And you are resolute?"

"I am! God being my helper, I will go forward in the path of duty. When I faint and fall by the way through weakness, the trial will end."

"Friends, wealth, social attractions - all that the world can give will be yours. But my way must be lonely - my heart desolate. I shall be" -

"Go, sir!" Miss Loring's voice was imperative, and there was a flash like indignation in her eyes. "Go sir!" she repeated. "This is unmanly!"

The last sentence stung Mr. Hendrickson, and he arose quickly. Miss Loring, who saw the effect of her words, threw up, with a woman's quick instinct, this further barrier between them -

"I marvel, sir, knowing, as you do, the sacred obligations under which I rest, that you should have dared utter language such as my ears have been compelled to hear this night! I take it as no compliment, sir."

The young man attempted to speak; but with a sternness of manner that sent a chill to his heart, she motioned him to be silent, and went on -

"Let this, sir, be the last time you venture to repeat what I cannot but regard as dis" -

Dishonorable was the word on her lips, but she suddenly checked herself. She could not say that to him.

Waking or sleeping, alone or in society, for weeks, months and years afterwards, the image of that young man's despairing face, as she saw it then, was ever before her.

"Insult! Dishonor!" he said, as if speaking to himself. "I could die for her - but not that! - not that!"

And without a parting glance or a parting word, Paul Hendrickson turned from the woman who was destined to influence his whole life, and left her alone in his bewilderment and wretchedness. It is difficult to say on which heart the heaviest pressure fell, or which life was most hopeless. It is alleged that only men die of broken hearts - that women can bear the crushing heel of disappointment, live on and endure, while men fall by the way, and perish in the strife of passion. It may be so. We know not. In the present case the harder lot was on Miss Loring. If she bore her pain with less of exterior token, it is no argument in favor of the lighter suffering. The patiently enduring oftenest bear the most.

T.S. Arthur

CHAPTER XI

THE efforts which were made to save Miss Loring, only had the effect to render the sacrifice more acutely painful. Evil instead of good followed Mrs. Denison's appeals to Mr. Dexter. They served but to arouse the demon jealousy in his heart. Upon Hendrickson's movements he set the wariest surveillance. Twice, since that never-to-be-forgotten evening he met the young man in company when Jessie was present. With an eye that never failed for an instant in watchfulness, he noted his countenance and movements; and he kept on his betrothed as keen an observation. Several times he left her alone, in order to give Hendrickson an opportunity to get into her company. But there was too studied avoidance of contact. Had they met casually and exchanged a few pleasant words, suspicion would have been allayed. As it was, jealousy gave its own interpretation to their conduct.

On the last of these occasions referred to, from a position where he deemed himself beyond the danger of casual observation, Hendrickson searched with his eyes for the object of his undying regard. He saw her, sitting alone, not far distant. Her manner was that of one lost in thought - the expression of her countenance dreamy, and overcast with a shade of sadness. How long he had been gazing upon her face, the young man could not have told, so absorbed was he in the feelings her presence had awakened, when turning almost involuntarily his eyes caught the gleam of another pair of eyes that were fixed intently upon him. So suddenly had he turned, that the individual observing him was left without opportunity to change in any degree the expression of his eyes or countenance. It was almost malignant. That individual was Leon Dexter.

In spite of himself, Hendrickson showed confusion, and was unable to return the steady gaze that rested upon him. His eyes fell. When he looked up again, which was in a moment, Dexter had left his position, and was crossing the room towards Miss Loring.

"It is the fiend Jealousy!" said Hendrickson, as he withdrew into another room. "Well - let it poison all the springs of his happiness, as he has poisoned mine! I care not how keen may be his sufferings."

He spoke with exceeding bitterness.

A few weeks later, and the dreaded consummation came. In honor of the splendid alliance formed by her niece, Mrs. Loring gave a most brilliant wedding party, and the lovely bride stood forth in all her beauty and grace - the admired and the envied. A few thought her rather pale - some said her eyes were too dreamy - and a gossip or two declared that the rich young husband had only gained her person, while her heart was in the keeping of another. "She has not married the man, but his wealth and position!" was the unguarded remark of one of these thoughtless individuals; and by a singular fatality, the sentence reached the ears of Mr. Dexter. Alas! It was but throwing another fagot on the already kindling fires of unhallowed jealousy. The countenance of the young husband became clouded; and it was only by an effort that he could arouse himself, and assume a gay exterior. The prize after which he had sprung with such eager haste, distancing all competitors, was now his own. Binding vows had been uttered, and the minister had said - "What God hath joined together, let not man put asunder." Yet, even in his hour of triumph, came the troubled conviction that, though he had gained the beautiful person of his bride, he could not say surely that her more beautiful soul was all his own.

And so there was a death's head at his feast; and the costly wine was dashed with bitterness.

Of what was passing in the mind of Dexter his bride had no knowledge; nor did her keen instincts warn her that the demon of jealousy was already in his heart. Suffering, and the colder spirit of endurance that followed, had rendered her, in a certain sense, obtuse in this direction.

A full-grown, strong woman, had Jessie become suddenly. The gentle, tenderly-loving, earnest, simple-hearted girl, could never have sustained the part it was hers to play. Unless a new and more vigorous life had been born in her, she must have fallen. But now she stood erect, shading her heart from her own eyes, and gathering from principle strength for duty. Very pure - very true she was. Yet, in her new relation, purity and truth were shrined in a cold exterior. It were not possible to be otherwise. She did not love her husband in any thing like the degree she was capable of loving. It was not in him to find the deep places of her heart. But true to him she could be, and true to him it was her purpose to remain.

Taking all the antecedents of this case, we will not wonder, when told that quite from the beginning of so inharmonious a union, Dexter found himself disappointed in his bride. He was naturally ardent and demonstrative; while, of necessity, she was calm, cold, dignified - or simply passive. She was never unamiable or capricious; and rarely opposed him in anything reasonable or unreasonable. But she was reserved almost to constraint at times - a vestal at the altar, rather than a loving wife. He was very proud of her, as well he might be; for she grew peerless in beauty. But her beauty was from the development of taste, thought, and intellect. It was not born of the affections. Yes, Leon Dexter was sadly disappointed. He wanted something more than all this.

Lifted from an almost obscure position, as the dependent niece of Mrs. Loring, the young wife of Mr. Dexter found herself in a larger circle, and in the society of men and women of more generally cultivated tastes. She soon became a centre of attraction; for taste attracts taste, mind seeks mind. And where beauty is added, the possessor has invincible charms. It did not escape the eyes of Dexter that, in the society of other men, his young wife was gayer and more vivacious (sic) that when with him. This annoyed him so much, that he began to act capriciously, as it seemed to Jessie. Sometimes he would require her to leave a pleasant company long before the usual hour, and sometimes he would refuse to go with her to parties or places of amusement, yet give no reasons that were satisfactory. On these occasions, a moody spirit would come over him. If she questioned, he answered with evasion, or covert ill-nature.

The closer union of an external marriage did not invest the husband with any new attractions for his wife. The more intimately she knew him, the deeper became her repugnance. He had no interior qualities in harmony with her own. An intensely selfish man, it was impossible for him to inspire a feeling of love in a mind so pure in its impulses, and so acute in its perceptions. If Mrs. Dexter had been a worldly-minded woman - a lover of - or one moved by the small ambitions of fashionable life - her husband would have been all well enough. She would have been adjoined to him in a way altogether satisfactory to her tastes, and they would have circled their orbit of life without an eccentric motion. But the deeper capacities and higher needs of Mrs. Dexter, made this union quite another thing. Her husband had no power to fill her soul - to quicken her life-pulses - to stir the silent chords of her heart with the deep, pure, ravishing melodies they were made to give forth. That she was superior to him mentally, Mr. Dexter was not long in discovering. Very rapidly did her mind, quickened by a never-dying pain, spring forward towards its culmination. Of its rapid growth in power and acuteness, he only had evidence when he listened to her in conversation with men and women of large acquirements and polished tastes. Alone with him, her mind seemed to grow duller every day; and if he applied the spur, it was only to produce a start, not a movement onwards.

Alas for Leon Dexter! He had caged his beautiful bird; but her song had lost, already, its ravishing sweetness.

CHAPTER XII

THE first year of trial passed. If the young wife's heart-history for that single year could be written, it would make a volume, every pages of which the reader would find (sic) spoted with his tears. No pen but that of the sufferer could write that history; and to her, no second life, even in memory, were endurable. The record is sealed up - and the story will not be told.

It is not within the range of all minds to comprehend what was endured. Wealth, position, beauty, admiration, enlarged intelligence, and highly cultivated tastes, were hers. She was the wife of a man who almost worshipped her, and who ceased not to woo her with all the arts he knew how to practise. Impatient he became, at times, with her impassiveness, and fretted by her coldness. Jealous of her he was always. But he strove to win that love which, ere his half-coercion of her into marriage, he had been warned he did not possess - but his strivings were in vain. He was a meaner bird, and could not mate with the eagle.

To Mrs. Dexter, this life was a breathing death. Yet with a wonderful power of endurance and self-control, she moved along her destined way, and none of the people she met in society - nor even her nearest friends - had any suspicion of her real state of mind. As a wife, her sense of honor was keen. From that virtuous poise, her mind had neither variableness nor shadow of turning. No children came with silken wrappings to hide and make softer the bonds that held her to

T.S. Arthur

her husband in a union that only death could dissolve; the hard, icy, galling links of the chain were ever visible, and their trammel ever felt. Cold and desolate the elegant home remained.

In society, Mrs. Dexter continued to hold a brilliant position. She was courted, admired, flattered, envied - the attractive centre to every circle of which she formed a part. Rarely to good advantage did her husband appear, for her mind had so far outrun his in strength and cultivation, that the contrast was seriously against him - and he felt it as another barrier between them.

One year of pride was enough for Mr. Dexter. A beautiful, brilliant, fashionable wife was rather a questionable article to place on exhibition; there was danger, he saw, in the experiment. And so he deemed it only the dictate of prudence to guard her from temptation. An incident determined him. They were at Newport, in the mid-season; and their intention was to remain there two weeks. They had been to Saratoga, where the beauty and brilliancy of Mrs. Dexter drew around her some of the most intelligent and attractive men there. All at once her husband suggested Newport.

"I thought we had fixed on next week," said Mrs. Dexter, in reply.

"I am not well," was the answer. "The sea air will do me good."

"We will go to-morrow, then," was the unhesitating response. Not made with interest or feeling; but promptly, as the dictate of wifely duty.

Just half an hour previous to this brief interview, Mr. Dexter was sitting in one of the parlors, and near him were two men, strangers, in conversation. The utterance by one of them of his wife's name, caused him to be on the instant all attention.

"She's charming!" was the response.

"One of the most fascinating women I have ever met! and my observation, as you know, is not limited. She would produce a sensation in Paris."

"Is she a young widow?"

"No - unfortunately."

"Who, or what is her husband?" was asked.

"A rich nobody, I'm told."

"Ah! He has taste."

"Taste in beautiful women, at least," was the rejoinder.

"Is he here?"

"I believe so. He would hardly trust so precious a jewel as that out of his sight. They say he is half-maddened by jealousy."

"And with reason, probably. Weak men, with brilliant, fashionable wives, have cause for jealousy. He's a fool to bring her right into the very midst of temptation."

"Can't help (sic) simelf, I presume. It might not be prudent to attempt the caging system."

A low, chuckling laugh followed. How the blood did go rushing and seething through the veins of Leon Dexter!

"I intend to know more of her," was continued. "Where do they live?"

"In B -"

"Ah! I shall be there during the winter."

T.S. Arthur

"She sees a great deal of company, I am told. Has weekly or monthly 'evenings' at which some of the most intellectual people in the city may be found."

"Easy of access, I suppose?"

"No doubt of it."

Dexter heard no more. On the next day he started with his wife for Newport. The journey was a silent one. They had ceased to converse much when alone. And now there were reasons why Mr. Dexter felt little inclination to intrude any common-places upon his wife.

They were passing into the hotel, on their arrival, when Mr. Dexter, who happened to be looking at his wife, saw her start, flush, and then turn pale. It was the work of an instant. His eyes followed the direction of hers, but failed to recognize any individual among the group of persons near them as the one who thus affected her by his presence. He left her in one of the parlors, while he made arrangements for rooms. In a few minutes he returned. She was sitting as he had left her, seeming scarcely to have stirred during his absence. Her eyes were on the floor, and when he said, "Come, Jessie!" she started and looked up at him, in a confused way.

"Our apartments are ready; come."

He had to speak a second time before she seemed to comprehend his meaning. She arose like one in deep thought, and moved along by her husband's side, leaving the parlor, and going up to the rooms which had been assigned to them. The change in her countenance and manner was so great, that her husband could not help remarking upon it.

"Are you not well, Jessie?" he asked, as she sat down with a weary air.

"Not very well," she answered - yet with a certain evasion of tone that repelled inquiry.

Mr. Dexter scanned her countenance sharply. She lifted her eyes at the moment to his face, and started slightly at the unusual meaning she saw therein. A flush betrayed her disturbed condition; and a succeeding pallor gave signs of unusual pain.

"Will you see a physician!"

"No - no!" she answered, quickly; "it was a momentary sickness - but is passing off now." She arose as she said this, and commenced laying aside her travelling garments. Mr. Dexter sat down, and taking a newspaper from his pocket, pretended to read; but his jealous eyes looked over the sheet, and rested with keen scrutiny on the face of his wife whenever it happened to be turned towards him. That she scarcely thought of his presence, was plain from the fact that she did not once look at him. Suddenly, as if some new thought had crossed his mind, Mr. Dexter arose, and after making some slight changes in his dress, left the apartment and went down stairs. He was evidently in search of some one; for he passed slowly, and with wary eyes, along the passages, porticos and parlors. The result was not satisfactory. He met several acquaintances, and lingered with each in conversation; but the watchful searching eyes were never a moment at rest.

The instant Mr. Dexter left the room, there was a change in his wife. The half indifferent, almost listless manner gave place to one that expressed deep struggling emotions. Her bent form became erect, and she stood for a little while listening with her eyes upon the door, as if in doubt whether her husband would not return. After the lapse of two or three minutes, she walked to the door, and placing her fingers on the key, turned it, locking herself in. This done, she retired slowly towards a lounge by the window, nearly every trace of excitement gone, and sitting down, was soon so entirely absorbed in thought as scarcely to show a sign of external life.

It was half an hour from the time Mr. Dexter left his wife, when he returned. His hand upon the lock aroused her from the waking dream into which she had fallen. As she arose, her manner began to change, and, ere she had reached the door, the quicker flowing blood was restoring the color to her cheeks. She had passed through a long and severe struggle; and woman's virtue, aided by woman's pride and will, had conquered.

Mrs. Dexter spoke to her husband cheerfully as he came in, and met his steady, searching look without a sign of confusion. He was at fault. Yet not deceived.

"Are you better?" he asked.

"Much better," she replied; and turning from him, went on with the arrangement of her toilet, which had been suspended from the period of her husband's absence, until his return. Mr. Dexter passed into their private parlor, adjoining the bedroom, and remained there until his wife had finished dressing.

"Shall we go down?" he inquired, as she came in looking so beautiful in his eyes that the very sight of her surpassing loveliness gave him pain. The Fiend was in his heart.

"Not now," she replied "I am still fatigued with the day's travel, and had rather not see company at present."

She glanced from the window.

"What a sublimity there is in the ocean!" she said, with an unusual degree of interest in her manner, when speaking to her husband. "I can never become so familiar with its grandeur and vastness, as to look upon its face without emotion. You remember Byron's magnificent apostrophe? -

"'Roll on, thou deep and dark blue ocean, roll.'"

And she repeated several of the stanzas from "Childe Harold," with an effect that stirred her husband's feelings more profoundly than they had ever been stirred by nature and poetry before.

"I have read and heard that splendid passage many times, but never with the meaning and power which your voice has lent to the poet's words," said Dexter, gazing with admiration upon his wife.

He sat down beside her, and took her hand in his. Her eyes wandered to his face, and lingered there as if she were searching the lineaments for a sign of something that her heart could take hold upon and cling to. And it was even so; for she felt that she needed strength and protection in an hour of surely coming trial. A feeble sigh and a drooping of the eyelids attested her disappointment. And yet as he leaned towards her she did not sit more erect, but rather suffered her body to incline to him. He still retained her hand, and she permitted him to toy with it, even slightly returning the pressure he gave.

"You shall be my teacher in the love of nature." He spoke with a glow of true feeling. "The lesson of this evening I shall never forget. Old ocean will always wear a different aspect in my eyes."

"Nature," replied Mrs. Dexter, "is not a mere dead symbol. - It is something more - an outbirth from loving principles - the body of a creating soul. The sea, upon whose restless surface we are gazing, is something more than a briny fluid, bearing ships upon its bosom - something more than a mirror for the arching heavens - something more than a symbol of immensity and eternity. There is a truth in nature far deeper, more divine, and of higher significance."

She paused, and for some moments her thoughts seemed floating away into a world, the real things of which our coarser forms but feebly represent.

"It must be so. I feel that it is so; yet what to you seems clear as the sunbeams, hides itself from me in dusky shadows. But say on Jessie. Your words are pleasant to my ears."

Mrs. Dexter seemed a little surprised at this language, for she turned her eyes from the sea to his face, and looked at him with a questioning gaze for some moments.

"This world is not the real world," she said, speaking earnestly and gazing at him intently to see how far his thought reflected hers.

"Is not this real?" Dexter asked, raising the hand of his wife and looking down upon it. "I call it a real hand."

"And I," said Mrs. Dexter, smiling, "call it only the appearance of a hand; it is the real hand that vitalizes and gives it power. This will decay - this appearance fade - but the real hand of my spirit will live on, immortal in its power as the human soul of which it makes a part."

"Into what strange labyrinths your mind is wandering Jessie!" said Mr. Dexter, a slight shade of disapproval in his voice. "I am afraid you are losing yourself."

"Rather say that I have been lost, and am finding myself in open paths, with the blue sky instead of forest foliage above me."

"Your language is a myth, Jessie. I never heard of your being lost. To me you have been ever present, walking in the sunlight, a divine reality. Not the mere appearance of a woman; but a *real* woman, and my wife. Pray do not lose yourself now! Do not recede from an actual flesh and blood existence into some world of dim philosophy whither I cannot go. I am not ready for your translation."

Mr. Dexter was half playful, half serious. His reply disappointed his wife. Her manner, warmer than usual, took on a portion of its old reserve. But she went on speaking.

"The immortal soul, spiritual in its essence, yet organized in all its minutest parts - cannot attain its full stature unless it receives immortal food. The aliments of mere sensual life are for the body, and the mind's lowest constituents of being; and they who are content to feed on husks must sort with the common herd. I have higher aspirations, my husband! I see within and above the animal and sensuous a real world of truth and goodness, where, and where only, the soul's immortal desires can be satisfied. With the key in my hand shall I not enter? The common air is too thick for me. I must perish or rise into purer atmospheres."

Mrs. Dexter paused, conscious that her husband did not appreciate her meanings. He was listening intently, and striving apparently after them; but to him only the things of sense were real; and he was not able to comprehend how lasting pleasure was to flow from the intellectual and spiritual. He did not answer, and she lapsed into silence; all the fine enthusiasm that had filled her countenance so full of a living beauty giving place to a cold, calm exterior. She had hoped to quicken her husband's sluggish perceptions, and to create in his mind an incipient love for the pure and beautiful things after which her own mind was beginning to aspire.

In her intercourse with refined and intellectual persons, Mrs. Dexter had made the acquaintance of a lady named Mrs. De Lisle. Her residence was not far from Mrs. Dexter's and they met often for pleasant and profitable conversation. In Mrs. De Lisle, Mrs. Dexter found a woman of not only superior attainments, but one possessing great purity of mind, and a high religious sense of duty. What struck her in the very beginning was a new mode of weighing human actions, and a quiet looking beneath the surface of things, and estimating all she saw by the quality within instead of by the appearance without. From the first, Mrs. Dexter was strongly attracted by this lady; and it was a little remarkable that her husband was as strongly repelled. He did not like her; and often spoke of her sneeringly as using an unknown tongue. His wife contended with him slightly at first in regard to Mrs. De Lisle; but soon

T.S. Arthur

ceased to notice his captious remarks.

In Mrs. De Lisle, the struggling and suffering young creature had found a true friend - not true in the sense of a weakly, sympathizing friend, but more really true; one who could lift her soul up into purer regions, and help it to acquire strength for duty.

There was another lady named Mrs. Anthony who had insinuated herself into the good opinion of Mrs. Dexter, and partially, also, into her confidence.

It does not take a quick-sighted woman long to comprehend the true marital standing of the friend in whom she feels an interest. Both Mrs. De Lisle and Mrs. Anthony soon discovered that no love was in the heart of Mrs. Dexter, and that consequently, no interior marriage existed. They saw also that Mr. Dexter was inferior, selfish, captious at times, and kept his wife always under surveillance, as if afraid of her constancy. The different conduct of the ladies, touching this relation of Mrs. Dexter to her husband, was in marked contrast. While Mrs. De Lisle never approached the subject in a way to invite communication, Mrs. Anthony, in the most adroit and insinuating manner, almost compelled a certain degree of confidence - or at least admission that there was not and never could be, any interior conjunction between herself and husband.

Mrs. Anthony was a highly intellectual and cultivated woman, with fascinating manners, a strong will, and singularly fine conversational powers. She usually exercised a controlling influence over all with whom she associated. Happy it was for Mrs. Dexter that a friend like Mrs. De Lisle came to her in the right time, and filled her mind with right principles for her own pure instincts to rest upon as an immovable foundation.

An hour spent in company with Mrs. Anthony always left Mrs. Dexter in a state of disquietude, and suffering from a sense of restriction and wrong. A feeling of alienation from her husband ever accompanied this state, and her spirit beat itself about, striking against the bars of conventional usage, until the bruised wings quivered wit hpain. But an hour spent with Mrs. De Lisle left her in a very different state. True thoughts were stirred, and the soul lifted upwards into regions of light and beauty. There was no grovelling about the earth, no fanning of selfish fires into smoky flames, no probing of half-closed wounds until the soul writhed in a new-born anguish - but instead, hopeful words, lessons of duty, and the introduction of an ennobling spiritual philosophy, that gave strength and tranquillity for the present, and promised the soul's highest fruition in the surely coming future.

Both Mrs. De Lisle and Mrs. Anthony were at Saratoga. The announcement of Mrs. Dexter that she was going to leave for Newport so suddenly surprised them both, as it had been understood that she was to remain for some time longer.

"My husband wishes to visit Newport now," was the answer of Mrs. Dexter to the surprised exclamation of Mrs. Anthony.

"Tell him that you wish to remain here," replied Mrs. Anthony.

"He is not well, and thinks the sea air will do him good."

"Not well! I met him an hour ago, and never saw him looking better in my life. Do you believe him?"

"Why not?" asked Mrs. Dexter.

Her friend laughed lightly, and then murmured -

"Simpleton! He's only jealous, and wants to get you away from your admirers. Don't go."

Mrs. Dexter laughed with affected indifference, but her color rose.

T.S. Arthur

"You wrong him," she said.

"Not I," was answered. "The signs are too apparent. I am a close observer, my dear Mrs. Dexter, and know the meaning of most things that happen to fall within the range of my observation. Your husband is jealous. The next move will be to shut you up in your chamber, and set a guard before the house. Now if you will take my advice, you'll say to this unreasonable lord and master of yours, 'Please to wait, sir, until I am ready to leave Saratoga. It doesn't suit me to do so just now. If you need the sea, run away to Newport and get a dash of old ocean. I require Congress water a little longer.' That's the way to talk, my little lady. But don't for Heaven's sake begin to humor his capricious fancies. If you do, it's all over."

Mrs. De Lisle was present, but made no remark. Mrs. Dexter parried her friend's admonition with playful words.

"Will you come to my room when disengaged?" said the former, as she rose to leave the parlor where they had been sitting.

"I will."

Mrs. De Lisle withdrew.

"You'll get a sermon on obedience to husbands," said Mrs. Anthony, tossing her head and smiling a pretty, half sarcastic smile. "I've one great objection to our friend."

"What is it?" inquired Mrs. Dexter.

"She's too proper."

"She's good," said Mrs. Dexter.

"I'll grant that; but then she's too good for me. I like a little wickedness sometimes. It's spicy, and gives a flavor to character."

Mrs. Anthony laughed one of her musical laughs. But growing serious in a moment, she said -

"Now, don't let her persuade you to humor that capricious husband of yours. You are something more than an appendage to the man. God gave you mind and heart, and created you an independent being. And a man is nothing superior to this, that he should attempt to lord it over his equal. I have many times watched this most cruel and exacting of all tyrannies, and have yet to see the case where the yielding wife could ever yield enough. Take counsel in time, my friend. Successful resistance now, will cost but a trifling effort."

Mrs. Dexter neither accepted nor repelled the advice; but her countenance showed that the remarks of Mrs. Anthony gave no very pleasant hue to her thoughts.

"Excuse me," she said rising, "I must see Mrs. De Lisle."

Mrs. Anthony raised her finger, and gave Mrs. Dexter a warning look, as she uttered the words -

"Don't forget."

"I won't," was answered.

Mrs. De Lisle received her with a serious countenance.

"You go to Newport in the morning?" she spoke, half-questioning and half in doubt.

"Yes."

The countenance of Mrs. De Lisle brightened.

"I thought," she said, after a pause, "that I knew you."

She stopped, as if in doubt whether to go on.

Mrs. Dexter looked into her face a moment.

"You understand me?" Mrs. De Lisle added.

"I do."

Mrs. Dexter betrayed unusual emotion.

"Forgive me," said her friend, "if I have ventured on too sacred ground. You know how deeply I am interested in you."

Tears filled the eyes of Mrs. Dexter; her lips quivered; every muscle of her face betrayed an inward struggle.

"Dear friend!" Mrs. De Lisle reached out her hands, and Mrs. Dexter leaned forward against her, hiding her face upon her breast. And now strong spasms thrilled her frame; and in weakness she wept - wept a long, long time. Nature had her way. But emotion spent itself, and a deep calm followed.

"Dear, patient, much-enduring, true-hearted friend!"

Mrs. De Lisle spoke almost in a whisper, her lips, close to the ear of Mrs. Dexter. The words, or at least some of them, had the effect to rouse the latter from her half lethargic condition. Lifting her face from the bosom of her friend, she looked up and said -

Patient? Much enduring?

"Is it not so? God give you wisdom, hope, triumph! I have looked into your heart many times, Mrs. Dexter. Not curiously, not as a study, not to see how well you could hide from common eyes its hidden anguish, but in deep and loving compassion, and with a strong desire to help and counsel. Will you admit me to a more sacred friendship?"

"Oh, yes! Gladly! Thankfully!" replied Mrs. Dexter. "How many, many times have I desired to open my heart to you; but dared not. Now, if you have its secret, gained by no purposed act of mine, I will accept the aid and counsel."

"You do not love," said Mrs. De Lisle - not in strong, emphatic utterance - not even calmly - but in a low, almost reluctant voice.

"I am capable of the deepest love," was answered.

"I know it."

"What then?" Mrs. Dexter spoke with some eagerness.

"You are a wife."

"I am," with coldness.

By your own consent?"

"It was extorted. But no matter. I accepted my present relation; and I mean to abide the contract. Oh, my friend! you know not the pain I feel in thus speaking, even to you. This is a subject over which I drew the veil of what I thought to be eternal silence. You have pushed it aside - not roughly, not with idle curiosity, but as a loving friend and counsellor. And now if you can impart strength or comfort, do so; for both are needed."

"The language of Mrs. Anthony pained me," said Mrs. De Lisle.

"Not more than it pained me," was the simple answer.

"And yet, Mrs. Dexter, though I observed you closely, I did not see the indignant flush on your face, that I had hoped to see mantling there."

"It was a simple schooling of the exterior. I felt that she was venturing on improper ground; but I did not care to let my

T.S. Arthur

real sentiments appear. Mrs. Anthony lacks delicacy in some things."

"Her remarks I regarded as an outrage. But seriously, Mrs. Dexter, is your husband so much inclined to jealousy?"

"I am afraid so."

"Do you think his purpose to leave Saratoga in the morning, springs from this cause?"

"I am not aware of any circumstance that should give rise to sudden apprehension in his mind. There is no one that I have remarked as offering me particular attentions. I am here, and cannot help the fact that gentlemen of superior taste, education, and high mental accomplishments, seem pleased with my society. I like to meet such persons - I enjoy the intercourse of mind with mind. It is the only compensating life I have. In it I forget for a little while my heart's desolation. In all that it is possible for me to be true to my husband, I am true; and I pray always that God will give me strength to endure even unto the end. His fears wrong me! There is not one of the scores of attractive men who crowd around me in public, who has the power, by look, or word, or action, to stir my heart with even the lightest throb of tender feeling. I have locked the door, and the key is hidden."

Mrs. De Lisle did not answer, for some time.

"Your high sense of honor, pure heart, and womanly perceptions, are guiding you right, I see!" she then remarked; "the ordeal is terrible, but you will pass through unscathed."

"I trust so!" was murmured in a sad voice; "I trust to keep my garments unspotted. Without blame, or suspicion of wrong, I cannot hope to move onward in my difficult way. Nor can I always hope to be patient under captious treatment, and intimations of unfaithfulness. The last will doubtless come; for when the fiend jealousy has enthroned itself in a man's heart, the most common-place actions may be construed into guilty concessions. All this will be deeply humiliating; and I know myself well enough to apprehend occasional indignant reactions, or cool defiances. I possess a high, proud spirit, which, if fairly aroused, is certain to lead me into stubborn resistance. So far I have managed to hold this spirit in abeyance; but if matters progress as they have begun, the climax of endurance will ere long be reached."

"Great circumspection on your part will be needed," said Mrs. De Lisle. "Remember always, your obligations as a wife. In consenting to enter into the most solemn human compact that is ever made, you assumed a position that gave you power over the happiness of another. If, as I gather from some things you have said, you went to the altar under constraint, an unloving bride, so much the more binding on you are the promises then made to seek your husband's happiness - even at the sacrifice of your own. In that act you wronged him - wronged him as no woman has a right to wrong any man, and you can never do enough by way of reparation."

"I was wronged," said Mrs. Dexter, her glance brightening, and a warmth, like indignation, in her voice; "for I was dragged to that marriage-altar against my will, and almost under protest. Mr. Dexter knew that my heart was not his."

"You were a free woman!" replied Mrs. De Lisle.

"I was not free," Mrs. Dexter answered.

"Not free? Who or what constrained you to such an act?"

"My honor. In a moment of weakness, and under the fascination of a strong masculine will, I plighted faith with Mr. Dexter. He knew at the time that I did not love him as a woman should love the man she consents to marry. He knew that he was extorting an unwilling consent. And just so far he took an unmanly advantage of a weak young girl. But the contract once made, truth and honor required its fulfillment.

T.S. Arthur

At least, so said my aunt, to whom alone I confided my secret; and so said my stern convictions of duty."

"So far from that," replied Mrs. De Lisle, "truth and honor required its non-fulfillment; for neither in truth nor in honor, could you take the marriage vows."

The directness with which Mrs. De Lisle stated this position of the case, startled her auditor.

"Is it not so?" was calmly asked. "You are too much in the habit of looking below the surface of things, to regard the formula of marriage as an unmeaning array of words. In their full signification, you could not utter the sentences you were required to speak - how then, as regarding truth and honor, could you pronounce them in that act of your life which, of all others, should have been most without guile? I would have torn all such extorted promises into a thousand tatters, and scattered them to the winds! The dishonor of breaking them were nothing to the wrong of fulfillment. Witness your unhappy lives!"

"Would to heaven you had been the friend of my girlhood!"

It was all the reply Mrs. Dexter made, as she bowed her head, like one pressed down by a heavy burden.

"You will now comprehend, more clearly than before," said Mrs. De Lisle, "your present duty to your husband. He thought that he was gaining a wife, and you, in wedding him promised to him to be a wife - promised with a deep conviction in your soul that the words were empty utterances. The case is a sad one, viewed in any aspect; but pardon me for saying, that you were most to blame. He was an ardent lover, whom you had fascinated; a man of superficial character, and not competent, at the time, to weigh the consequences of an act he was so eager to precipitate. To possess, he imagined was to enjoy. But you were better versed in the heart's lore, and knew he would wake up, ere many moons had passed, to the sad discovery that what he had wooed as substance was only a cheating shadow. And he is waking up. Every day he is becoming more and more clearly convinced that you do not love him, and can never be to him the wife he had fondly hoped to gain. Have you not laid upon yourself a binding obligation? Is it a light thing so to mar the whole life of man? Your duty is plain, Mrs. Dexter. Yield all to him you can, and put on towards him always the sunniest aspects and gentlest semblances of your character. If he is capricious, humor him; if suspicious, act with all promptness in removing suspicion to the extent of your power. Make soft the links of the chain that binds you together, with downy coverings. Truth, honor, duty, religion, all require this."

"Dear friend!" said Mrs. Dexter, grasping the hand of Mrs. De Lisle, "you have lifted me out of a thick atmosphere, through which my eyes saw everything in an uncertain light, up into a clear seeing region. Yes, truth, honor, duty, religion, all speak to my convictions; and with all the truth that in me lieth, will I obey their voice. But love is impossible, and its semblance in me is so faint that my husband cannot see the likeness. There lies the difficulty. He wants a fond, tender, loving wife - a pet and a plaything. These he can never find in me; for, Heaven help me! Mrs. De Lisle, his sphere grows more and more repulsive every day, and I shudder sometimes at the thought of unmitigated disgust!"

"Do your best, my friend," was the answer of of Mrs. De Lisle. "Fill, to the utmost of your ability, all your wifely relations, and seek to develop in your husband those higher qualities of thought and feeling to which your spirit can attach itself. And above all, do not listen to such erroneous counsels as Mrs. Anthony gave just now. If followed they will surely produce a harvest of misery."

"Thanks, good counsellor! I will heed your words. They come in the right time, and strengthen my better purposes," said Mrs. Dexter. "To-morrow I shall leave with my husband for Newport, and he shall see in me no signs of reluctance. Nor do

T.S. Arthur

I care, except to leave your company. I will find as much to keep my thoughts busy at Newport as here."

CHAPTER XIII

THE effort to interest her husband in things purely intellectual failed, and a shade of disappointment settled on the feelings of Mrs. Dexter. She soared, altogether, too far up into the mental atmosphere for him. He thought her ideal and transcendental; and she felt that only the sensual principles in his mind were living and active. Conversation died between them, and both relapsed into that abstracted silence - musing on one side and moody on the other - which filled so large a portion of their time when together.

"Shall we go down to the parlors?" said Mr. Dexter, rousing himself. "The afternoon is running away fast towards evening."

"I am more fatigued than usual," was answered, "and do not care to make my appearance before tea-time. You go down; and I will occupy myself with a book. When the tea-bell rings, I will wait for you to come and escort me to the table."

Mr. Dexter did not urge his wife to leave their rooms, but went down as she had suggested. The moment he left her, there occurred a great change in her whole appearance. She was sitting on a lounge by the window. Instead of rising to get a book, or seeking for any external means of passing a solitary hour, she shrunk down in her seat, letting her eyes droop gradually to the floor. At first, her countenance was disturbed; but its aspect changed to one of deep abstraction. And thus she sat for nearly an hour. The opening of her room door startled her into a life of external (sic) conciousness. Her husband

T.S. Arthur

entered. She glanced at his face, and saw that something had occurred to ruffle his feelings. He looked at her strangely for some moments, as if searching for expected meanings in her countenance.

"Are you not well?" Mrs. Dexter asked.

"Oh, yes, I'm well enough," he answered with unusual abruptness of manner.

She said no more, and he commenced pacing the floor of their small parlor backwards and forwards with restless footsteps.

Once, without moving her head or body, Mrs. Dexter stole a glance towards her husband; she encountered his eyes turning stealthily upon her, and scanning her face with an earnest scrutiny. A moment their eyes lingered, mutually spell-bound, and then the glances were mutually withdrawn. Mr. Dexter continued his nervous perambulations, and his wife remained seated and silent.

The ringing of the bell announced tea. Mr. Dexter paused, and Mrs. Dexter, rising without remark, took his arm, and they went down to the dining-hall, neither of them speaking a word. On taking her place at the table, Mrs. Dexter's eyes ran quickly up and down the lines of faces opposite.

This was done with so slight a movement of the head, that her husband, who was on the alert, did not detect the rapid observation. For some three or four minutes the guests came filing in, and all the while Mrs. Dexter kept glancing from face to face. She did not move her head or seem interested in the people around her; but her eyes told a very different story. Twice the waiter asked if she would take tea or coffee, before she noticed him, and her answer, "Coffee," apprised her watchful husband of the fact that she was more than usually lost in thought.

"Not coffee?" Mr. Dexter bent to his wife's ear.

"No, black tea," she said, quickly, partly turning to the waiter. "I was not thinking," she added, speaking to her husband. At the moment Mrs. Dexter turned towards the waiter, she leaned forward, over the table, and gave a rapid glance down at the row of faces on that side; and in replying to her husband, she managed to do the same thing for the other end of the table. No change in her countenance attested the fact that her search for some desired or expected personage had been successful. The half emptied cup of tea, and merely broken piece of toast lying on her plate, showed plainly enough that either indisposition or mental disturbance, had deprived her of appetite.

From the tea table they went to one of the parlors. Only a few gentlemen and ladies were there, most of the guests preferring a stroll out of doors, or an evening drive.

"Shall we ride? It is early yet, and the full moon will rise as the sun goes down."

"I have ridden enough to day," Mrs. Dexter answered. "Fatigue has made me nervous. But don't let that prevent your taking a drive."

"I shall not enjoy it unless you are with me," said Mr. Dexter.

"Then I will go." Mrs. Dexter did not speak fretfully, nor in the martyr tone we often hear, but in a voice of unexpected cheerfulness. "Order the carriage," she added, as she rose; "I will get my bonnet and shawl, and join you here by the time it is at the door."

"No - no, Jessie! Not if you are so fatigued. I had forgotten our journey to-day," interposed Mr. Dexter.

"A ride in the bracing salt air will do me good, perhaps. I am, at least, disposed to make the trial. So order the carriage, and I will be with you in a moment."

Mrs. Dexter spoke with a suddenly outflashing animation, and then left her husband to make preparations for accompanying him in the drive. She had passed through the parlor door on to one of the long porticoes of the building, and was moving rapidly, when, just before reaching the end, where another door communicated with a stairway, she suddenly stood still, face to face with a man who had stepped from that door out upon the portico.

"Jess - Mrs. Dexter!" the man checked the unguarded utterance of her familiar Christian name, and gave the other designation.

"Mr. Hendrickson!"

Only for an instant did Mrs. Dexter betray herself; but in that instant her heart was read, as if a blaze of lightning had flashed over one of its pages, long hidden away in darkness, and revealed the writing thereon in letters of gleaming fire.

"You arrived to day?" Mr. Hendrickson also regained the even balance of mind which had momentarily been lost, and regained it as quickly as the lady. He spoke with the pleased air of an acquaintance - nothing more.

"This afternoon," replied Mrs. Dexter in a quiet tone, and with a smile in which no casual observer could have seen anything deeper than pleasant recognition.

"How long will you remain?"

"It is not certain; perhaps until the season closes."

Mrs. Dexter made a motion to pass on. Mr. Hendrickson raised his hat and bowed very respectfully; and thus the sudden interview ended.

Mr. Dexter had followed his wife to the door of the parlor, and stood looking at her as she retired along the portico. This meeting with Hendrickson was therefore in full view. A sudden paleness overspread his countenance; and from his convulsed lips there fell a bitter imprecation.

On reaching her apartments, Mrs. Dexter was so weak that she was forced to sit down upon the first chair she could obtain. A dead pallor was in her face.

"Oh, give me strength - self control - motives to duty!" - in weakness and fear her quivering heart cried upwards.

"Jessie!" How long she had been sitting thus Mrs. Dexter knew not. She started. It was the voice of her husband.

"Not ready yet, I see!" His tones were rough - his manner excited. "And the carriage has stood at the door for ten minutes."

"I am ready!" she answered, starting up, and lifting her bonnet from the bed.

"It is no matter now. The sun is setting, and I have ordered the carriage back to the stable. You only consented to go on my account; and I am impatient under mere acquiescence."

"You wrong me, Mr. Dexter," said his wife, with (sic) unusal earnestness of manner. "I am ready to go with you at all times; and I strive in all things to give you pleasure. Did I hesitate a moment when you suddenly declared your wish to leave Saratoga for Newport?"

"No, of course you did not; for you were too glad of the opportunity to get here." There was a strange gleam in the eyes of Mr. Dexter as he said this; and his voice had in it an angry bitterness never before observed.

"What do you mean, sir?" demanded the outraged wife, turning upon her husband abruptly, and showing an aspect so stern and fierce, that the astonished man retreated a pace or two as if in fear. Never before had he seen in that beautiful face the reflection of a spirit so wildly disturbed by passion.

"Speak out, Leon Dexter! What do you mean?"

And her eyes rested on his with a glance as steady as an eagle's.

"I saw your meeting a little while ago."

Mr. Dexter rallied a little.

"What meeting?" There was no betraying sign in Mrs. Dexter's face, nor the least faltering in her tones.

"Your meeting with *him*."

"With whom? Speak out plainly, sir! I am in no mood for trifling, and in no condition for solving riddles."

"With Paul Hendrickson." Dexter pronounced the name slowly, and with all the meaning emphasis he could throw into his voice.

"Well, sir, what of that?" Still neither eye nor voice faltered.

"Much! You see that I understand you!"

"I see that you do not understand me," was firmly answered. "And now, sir, will you suffer me to demand an explanation of your language just now. I want no evasion - no faltering - no holding back. 'Too glad of an opportunity to get here!' That was the sentence. Its meaning, sir?"

The small head of Mrs. Dexter was erect; her nostrils distended; her lips closely laid upon each other; her eyes full fixed and almost fiery in their intense light. Suddenly she was transformed in the eyes of her husband from a yielding, gentle, though cold woman into the very spirit of accusation and defiance. He was silent; for he saw that he had gone too far.

"That must be explained, sir!" She was not to be turned aside. "I have noted your capricious conduct; your singular glances at times; your strange moodiness without apparent cause. A little light has given a faint impression of their meaning. But I must have the full blaze of your thoughts. Nothing else will satisfy me now."

She paused. Mr. Dexter had indeed gone a step too far, a fact of which he was painfully aware. He had conjured up a spirit that it might not be easy to lay.

"You are too excited. Calm yourself," he said.

Turning from her husband, Mrs. Dexter crossed the room, and seating herself upon a sofa, said, in a quiet way -

"Sit down beside me, Mr. Dexter. I am calm. Sit down and speak; for your recent language must be explained. Evasion will be fruitless - I will not accept of it."

"I spoke hastily. Forget my words."

Mr. Dexter sat down beside his wife, and spoke in a gentle soothing manner.

"It is all in vain, Mr. Dexter! All in vain! Yours were no idle words; and I can never forget them. You have greatly misapprehended your wife, I see; and the quicker you know this the better it will be for both of us. The time has come for explanation - and it shall be made! Why did I wish to come to Newport?"

"You knew that Paul Hendrickson was here," said Mr. Dexter; "that was the reason!"

"It is false, sir!" was the quick and sharp rejoinder.

"Jessie! beware how you speak!" The angry blood mounted to the very brow of the husband.

T.S. Arthur

"It is false, sir!" she repeated, even more emphatically, if that were possible. "Of his movements I am as ignorant as you are!"

"I cannot tamely bear such words," said Mr. Dexter, still much excited.

"And *I will not* bear such imputations," was firmly rejoined.

Mr. Dexter arose, and commenced the unsatisfactory movement of pacing the floor. Mrs. Dexter remained sitting firmly erect, her eyes following the form of her husband.

"We will drop the subject now and forever," said the former, stopping, at length, in front of his wife.

Mrs. Dexter did not reply.

"I may have been too hasty."

"*May* have been!" There was contempt on the lip, and indignation in the voice of Mrs. Dexter.

"Yes, *may*. We are certain of nothing in this world," said her husband, coldly; "and now, as I said, we will drop the subject."

"It is easier to say than to unsay, Mr. Dexter. The sentiment is very trite, but it involves a world of meaning sometimes, and" - she paused, then added, with marked emphasis - "*does now!*"

Mr. Dexter made no response, and there the matter ended for the time; each of the ill-assorted partners farther from happiness than they had yet been since the day of their unfortunate union.

CHAPTER XIV

AN hour later: Scene, the public parlor.

"Mrs. Dexter."

The lady rose, a pleasant smile animating her face, and returned the gentleman's courteous greeting.

"Mr. Hendrickson." Yes, that was the name on her lips.

"You arrived to-day," he said, and he took a place at the other end of the *tete-a-tete*.

"Yes."

"From Saratoga, I believe?"

"Yes. How long have you been at Newport?"

"I arrived only this morning. You are looking very well, Mrs. Dexter."

"Am I?"

"Yes. Time lays his hands upon you lightly!"

The shadow of another's presence came between them.

"Mr. Dexter, my husband; Mr. Hendrickson, from B -," said

T.S. Arthur

Mrs. Dexter, with the most perfect ease of manner, presenting the two gentlemen. They had met before, as the reader knows, and had good reason for remembering each other. They touched hands, Dexter frowning, and Hendrickson slightly embarrassed. Mrs. Dexter entirely herself, smiling, talkative, and with an exterior as unruffled as a mountain lake.

"How long will you remain?" she asked, speaking to Mr. Hendrickson.

"Several days."

"Ah! I am pleased to hear you say so. I left some very pleasant friends at Saratoga, but yours is the only familiar face I have yet seen here."

"I saw Mr. and Mrs. Florence just now," said Mr. Dexter.

"Did you?"

"Yes. There they are, at the lower end of the parlor. Do you see them?"

Mrs. Dexter turned her eyes in the direction indicated by her husband, and replied in an indifferent manner:

"Oh, yes."

"Mrs. Florence is looking at you now. Won't you go over and see her?"

"After a while," replied Mrs. Dexter. Then turning to Mr. Hendrickson, she said:

"These summer resorts are the dullest places imaginable without congenial friends."

"So I should think. But you can scarcely know the absence of these. I heard of you at Saratoga, as forming the centre of one of the most agreeable and intelligent circles there."

"Ah!" Mrs. Dexter was betrayed into something like surprise.

"Yes. I saw Miss Arden in New York, as I came through. She had been to Saratoga."

"Miss Arden? I don't remember her," said Mrs. Dexter.

"She resides in B -."

"Miss Arden? Miss Arden?" Mrs. Dexter seemed curious. "What is her appearance?"

"Tall, with a very graceful figure. Complexion dark enough to make her pass for a brunette. Large black eyes and raven hair."

"In company with her mother?" said Mrs. Dexter.

"Yes."

"I remember her now. She was quite the belle at Saratoga. But I was not so fortunate as to make her acquaintance. She sings wonderfully. Few professional artists are so gifted."

"You have used the right word," said Mr. Hendrickson. "Her musical powers are wonderful. I wish you knew her, she is a charming girl."

"You must help me to that knowledge on our return to B -."

"Nothing would give me more pleasure. I am sure you will like each other," said Hendrickson, warmly.

From that point in the conversation Mrs. Dexter began to lose her self-possession, and free, outspoken manner. The subject was changed, but the airiness of tone and lightness of speech was gone. Just in time, Mrs. Florence came across the room, joined the circle, and saving her from a betrayal of feelings that she would not, on any account, have manifested.

Mrs. Florence was a woman of taste. She had been in New York a few days previously, whither she had gone to hear a celebrated European singer, whose fame had preceded her. Her allusion to this fact led to an introduction of the subject of music. Hendickson made some remarks that arrested her attention, when quite an animated conversation sprung up between them. Mrs. Dexter did not join in it; but sat a closely observant listener. The young man's criticisms on the art of music surprised her. They were so new, so analytical, and so comprehensive. He had evidently studied the subject, not as an artist, but as a philosopher - but with so clear a comprehension of the art, that from the mere science, he was able to lead the mind upward into the fullest appreciation of the grander ideal.

Now and then as he talked, Mr. Dexter passed in a brief sentence; but to the keen, intelligent perception of his wife, what mere sounding words were his empty common-places! The contrast between him and Hendrickson was painful. It was in vain that she tried not to make this contrast. It thrust itself upon her, in spite of all resistance.

Mr. Florence had crossed the room with his wife, and joined the little circle. He did not take part in the conversation, and now said, rising as he spoke.

"Come, Dexter; let's you and I have a game of billiards."

He laid his band familiarly on the arm of Mr. Dexter, and that individual could not refuse to accept the invitation. They left the room together. This withdrawal of Mr. Dexter put both his wife and Mr. Hendrickson more at their ease. Both felt his absence as a relief. For a time the conversation was chiefly conducted by the latter and Mrs. Florence, only an occasional remark falling from the lips of Mrs. Dexter, and that almost extorted by question or reference. But gradually she was drawn in, and led on, until she was the talker and they the listeners.

When interested in conversation, a fine enthusiasm always gave to the manners of Mrs. Dexter a charming grace, and to her beautiful countenance a higher beauty. She was almost fascinating. Never had Hendrickson felt her power as he felt it now, while looking into her animated face, and listening to sentiment, description, criticism or anecdote, flowing from her lips in eloquent language, and evincing a degree of taste, discrimination, refinement and observation he could scarcely have imagined in one of her age.

He was leaning towards her, and listening with rapt interest, his countenance and eyes full of admiration, when a quick, impatient *ahem* caused him to look up. As he did so, he encountered the severe face and piercing eyes of Mr. Dexter. The sudden change in the expression of his countenance warned Mrs. Dexter of the presence of her husband, who had approached quietly, and was standing a pace or two behind his wife. But not the slightest consciousness of this presence did her manner exhibit. She kept on talking as before, and talking to Mr. Hendrickson.

"Will you go with me now, Mrs. Dexter?" said her husband, coming forward, and making a motion as if about to offer his arm.

"Not yet if you please, Mr. Dexter," was smilingly answered. "I am too much interested in this good company. Come, sit down here," and she made room for him on the sofa.

But he stood still.

"Then amuse yourself a little longer," said his wife, in a gay voice. "I will be ready to go with you after a while."

Mr. Dexter moved away, disappointed, and commenced pacing the floor of the long parlor. At every turn his keen eyes took in the aspect of the little group, and particularly the meaning of his wife's face, as it turned to Mr. Hendrickson, either in the play of expression or warm with the listener's

T.S. Arthur

interest. The sight half maddened him. Three times, in the next half hour, he said to his wife, as he paused in his restless promenade before her -

"Come, Jessie."

But she only threw him a smiling negative, and became still more interesting to her friends. At last, and of her own will, she arose, and bowing, with a face all smiles and eyes dancing in light, to Mr. Hendrickson and Mrs. Florence, she stepped forward, and placing her hand on the arm of her husband, went like a sunbeam from the room.

CHAPTER XV

"MADAM!"

They had reached their own apartments, and Mrs. Dexter was moving forward past her husband. The stern imperative utterance caused her to pause and turn round.

"We leave for home in the morning!" said Mr. Dexter.

"*We?*" His wife looked at him fixedly as she made the simple interrogation.

"Yes, *we!*" was answered, and in the voice of one who had made up his mind, and did not mean to be thwarted in his purpose.

"Mr. Dexter!" his wife stood very erect before him; her eyes did not quail beneath his angry glances; nor was there any sign of weakness in her low, even tones. "Let me warn you now - and regard the warning as for all time - against any attempt to coerce me into obedience to your arbitrary exactions. Your conduct to-night was simply disgraceful - humiliating to yourself, and mortifying and unjust to your wife. Let us have no more of this. There is a high wall between us, Mr. Dexter - high as heaven and deep as -." Her feelings were getting the rein and she checked herself. "Your own hands have built it," she resumed in a colder tone, "but your own hands, I fear, have not the strength to pull it down. Love you I never did, and you knew it from the beginning; love you I never can.

That is a simple impossibility. But true to you as steel to the magnet in all the externals of my life, I have been and shall continue to be, even to the end of this unhappy union. As a virtuous woman, I could be nothing less. The outrage I have suffered this day from your hands, is irreparable. I never imagined it would come to this. I did not dream that it was in you to charge upon your wife the meditation of a crime the deepest it is possible for a woman to commit. That you were weakly jealous, I saw; and I came here in cheerful acquiescence to your whim, in order to help you to get right. But this very act of cheerful acquiescence was made the ground of a charge that shocked my being to the inmost and changed me towards you irrevocably."

The stern angry aspect of Mr. Dexter was all gone. It seemed as if emotion had suddenly exhausted itself.

"We had better go home to-morrow." He spoke in a subdued voice. "Neither of us can find enjoyment here."

"I shall not be ready to morrow, nor the next day either," was the out-spoken reply. "To go thus hurriedly, after your humiliating exhibition of distrust, would only be to give free rein to the tongue of scandal; and that I wish to avoid."

"It has free rein already," said Mr. Dexter. "At Saratoga I heard your name lightly spoken and brought you away for that very reason. You are not chary enough of yourself in these public places. I know men better than you do."

"If a light word was spoken of me, sir, at Saratoga or anywhere else, you alone are to blame. My conduct has warranted no such freedom of speech. But I can easily imagine how men will think lightly of a woman when her husband shows watchfulness and suspicion. It half maddens me, sir, to have this disgrace put upon me. To-morrow week I will go home if you then desire it - not a day earlier. And I warn you against any more such exhibitions as we have had to-night. If you cannot take pleasure in society that is congenial to my taste, leave me to my enjoyment, but don't mar it with your cloudy presence. And set this down as a truism - the wife that must be watched, is not worth having."

For utterances like these, Mr. Dexter was not prepared. They stunned and weakened him. He felt that he had a spirit to deal with that might easily be driven to desperation. A man, if resolute, he had believed might control the actions of almost any woman - that woman being his wife. And he had never doubted the result of marital authority, should he at any time deem it necessary to lay upon Mrs. Dexter an iron hand. The occasion, as he believed, had arrived; the hand was put forth; the will was resolute; but his vice-like grip closed upon the empty air! The spirit with which he had to deal was of subtler essence and more vigorous life than he had imagined.

How suddenly were Mrs. Dexter's wifely, unselfish and self-denying purposes in regard to her husband scattered upon the winds! She had come to Newport, resolved to be all to him that it was possible for her to be - even to the withdrawing of herself more from social circles in which attractive men formed a part. The admonitions of Mrs. De Lisle sunk deeply into her heart. She saw her relation to her husband in a new aspect. He had larger claims upon her than she had admitted heretofore. If she had been partly coerced into the compact, he had been deceived by her promises at the altar into expecting more than it was in her power to give. She owed him not only a wife's allegiance, but a wife's tender consideration.

Alas! how suddenly had all these good purposes been withered up, like tender flowers in the biting frost! And now there was strife between them - bitterness, anger, scorn, alienation. The uneasiness which her husband had manifested for some months previously, whenever she was in free, animated conversation with gentlemen, annoyed her slightly; but she had never regarded it as a very serious affection on his part, and, conscious of her own purity, believed that he would ere long see the evidence thereof, and cease to give himself useless trouble. His conduct at Saratoga, followed by the conversations with Mrs. De Lisle and Mrs. Anthony, aroused her to a truer sense of his actual state of mind. His singular, stealthy scanning of her countenance, immediately after their arrival at Newport, following, as she rightly concluded, his unexpected meeting with Hendrickson, considerably disturbed the balance of mind she had sought to gain, and this dimmed her clear perceptions of duty. His direct reference to Mr. Hendrickson, after her hurried meeting with him, filled her with indignation, and simply prepared the way for this last defiant position. She felt deeply outraged, and wholly estranged.

Icy reserve and distant formality now marked the intercourse of Mr. and Mrs. Dexter. It was all in vain that he sought to win back that semblance of affection which he had lost. Mrs. Dexter was too sincere a woman - too earnest and true - for broad disguises. She could be courteous, regardful, attentive to all the needs of her husband; but she could not pretend to love, when daily her heart experienced new occasions of dislike.

On the next morning, Mrs. Dexter, on going into one of the parlors, met Mr. Hendrickson. From his manner, it was evident that he had been waiting there in hopes to gain an interview. Mrs. Dexter felt displeased. She was a lawful wife, and it struck her as an implication on his part of possible dishonor on hers. He came forward to meet her as she entered the room, with a pleased smile on his face, but she gave his warm greeting but a cold return. An instant change in his manner, showed the effect upon his feelings.

"I shall leave to-day," he said.

"So soon? I thought you purposed remaining for several days."

"So I did. But I have a letter this morning from the brother of Miss Arden, of whom I spoke last evening. He leaves her at Albany to-day, and asks me to join her to-morrow. They were on their way to Niagara; but unexpected business - he is a lawyer - requires him to return home; and I am to be the young lady's escort. So they have arranged the matter, and I cannot decline, of course."

"Why should you?" Mrs. Dexter schooled her voice. Its natural expression, at that time, might have betrayed a state of feeling that it would have been treason to exhibit.

"True. Why should I? The lady is charming. I was going to say that she has not her peer."

"Why not say it?" remarked Mrs. Dexter.

"Because," replied Mr. Hendrickson, as his eyes withdrew themselves from the face of Mrs. Dexter, "I do not believe it. She has her peer."

"She must be a lovely woman so to captivate your fancy," said Mrs. Dexter.

"Did I say that she had captivated my fancy?" asked Hendrickson.

"If not in so many formally spoken words, yet in a language that we ladies can read at a glance," replied Mrs. Dexter, affecting a gay smile. "Well," she added, "as you are to be so largely the gainer by this sudden withdrawal from Newport, we quiet people, who cannot but miss your pleasant company, have nothing left but acquiescence. I hope to make Miss Arden's acquaintance on our return to B -."

The voice of Mrs. Dexter had a faint huskiness and there were signs of depression which she was not able to conceal. These the watchful eyes of Mr. Hendrickson detected. But so far from taking any advantage thereof, he made an effort to divert both her mind and his own by the introduction of a more indifferent subject. They conversed for half an hour longer, but no further reference was made to Miss Arden. Then Mr. Hendrickson excused himself. Mrs. Dexter did not see him again.

He left for Boston soon after, on his way to join Miss Arden at Albany.

From the parlor Mrs. Dexter returned to her own rooms, and did not leave them during the day. She had felt feverish on rising, and was conscious of a pressure on the brain, accompanied by a feeling of lassitude that was unusual. This condition of the system increased, as the day wore on. At dinner-time, her husband urged her to go with him to the table; but she had a loathing for food, and declined. He ordered a servant to take tea, with toast and some delicacies, to her room; but when he came up again, he found them untasted.

"Was this a disease of mind or body?" Mr. Dexter asked himself the question, and studied over the solution. Notwithstanding the disturbed interview with his wife on the previous evening, he had kept his eyes on her, and noticed her meeting with Hendrickson in the parlor. Her warning, however, had proved effectual in preventing his intrusion upon them. He saw Hendrickson leave her, and noticed that she sat in deep abstraction for some time afterwards, and that when she arose, and went up to her own apartments, her face wore an expression that was unusual. Much to his surprise, he saw Hendrickson leave soon after for Boston. On examining the register, he learned that his destination was Albany.

A momentary relief was experienced at this departure; but soon mystery was suggested, and a mutual understanding between his wife and Hendrickson imagined. And so fuel was heaped on the fires of jealousy, which blazed up again as fiercely as ever. The seclusion of herself in her own room by Mrs. Dexter, following as it did immediately on the departure of Hendrickson, confirmed him in the impression that she was deeply interested in her old lover. How else could he interpret her conduct? If she were really sick, conflict of feeling, occasioned by his presence, was the cause. That to his mind was clear. And he was not so far wrong; for, in part, here lay the origin of her disturbed condition of mind and body. Still, his conclusions went far beyond the truth.

Mrs. Dexter was lying on the bed when her husband came up from dinner. She did not stir on his entrance. Her face was turned away, and partly hidden by the fringe of a pillow.

"You must eat something," he said, speaking kindly. But she neither moved nor replied.

"Jessie." No motion or response.

"Jessie!" Mr. Dexter stood a few feet from the bed, looking at her.

"She may be sleeping," he thought, and stepping forward, he bent down and laid his fingers lightly on her cheek. It was unnaturally hot. "Jessie" - he uttered her name again - "are you asleep?"

"No." She replied in a feeble murmur.

"Won't you have a cup of tea?"

"No."

"Are you sick?"

She did not answer. He laid his hand upon her cheek again.

"You have fever."

A low sigh was the only response.

"Does your head ache?"

Something was said in reply, but the ear of Mr. Dexter could not make out the words.

T.S. Arthur

"Jessie! Jessie! Why don't you answer me? Are you sick?"

Mr. Dexter spoke with rising impatience. Still and silent as an effigy she remained. For a moment or two he strode about the room, and then went out abruptly. He came back in half an hour.

There lay his wife as he had left her, and without the appearance of having stirred. A shadow of deeper concern now fell upon his spirits. Bending over the bed, and laying his hand upon her face again, he perceived that it was not only flushed, but hotter than before. He spoke, but her ears seemed shut to his voice.

"Jessie! Jessie!" He moved her gently, turning her face towards him. Her eyes were closed, her lips shut firmly, and wearing an expression of pain, her forehead slightly contracted.

"Shall I call a physician?" he asked.

But she did not reply. Sudden alarm awakened in the heart of Mr. Dexter. Going to the bell, he rang it violently. To the servant who came he said, hurriedly -

"Go and find Dr. G - , and tell him that I wish to see him immediately."

The servant departed, and Dexter went back to the bed. No change had occurred in his wife. She still lay, to all appearance, in a stupor. It was nearly a quarter of an hour before Dr. G - came; the waiter had been at some trouble to find him.

"My wife seems quite ill," said Mr. Dexter, as he entered, "and, I think requires medical attention."

Dr. G - went to the bedside and stood looking at the flushed face of Mrs. Dexter for some moments. Then he laid his hand against her cheek, and then took hold of her wrist. Mr. Dexter, whose eyes were on him, thought he saw him start and change countenance at the first stroke of the pulse that played against his fingers.

"How long has she been in this condition?" asked the doctor, turning with a serious aspect to Mr. Dexter.

"She has not seemed well since morning" was replied. "I noticed that she scarcely tasted food at breakfast, and she has kept her room for most of the day, lying down for a greater part of the time. I left her on the bed when I went to dinner. She did not complain of indisposition, but seemed listless and out of spirits. I ordered tea sent up, but, as you perceive, it has not been tasted. On my return, I found her in the condition in which she now lies - (sic)appparently in a heavy sleep."

The physician did not seem to get any light from this statement. He turned his eyes again upon the face of Mr. Dexter, and stood in thought for almost a minute. Then he examined her pulse again. It had a strong, rapid, wiry beat. Stooping, he looked very closely at the condition of her skin; then shook his head, and said something in an under tone.

"Do you think her seriously ill?" inquired Mr. Dexter.

"Has there been any unusual exposure; or any strong mental disturbance?" asked the doctor, not seeming to have heard the question.

"There has been mental disturbance," said Mr. Dexter.

"Of a violent character?"

"She was strongly agitated last night, at something that happened."

"Was it of a nature to leave a permanent impression on her feelings?"

"Yes." The answers were made with evident reluctance.

"Her condition is an unusual one," said the doctor, musing; and he resumed his examination of the case.

"Dr. R -, from Boston, arrived to-day;" he looked up, and presented a very grave face to the now seriously alarmed husband. "I think he had better be consulted."

"Oh, by all means," said Mr. Dexter. "Shall I go in search of him?"

"Do you know (sic) kim?"

"I do not."

"I will go then. It may save time, and that is important."

The doctor went out hurriedly, and in less than five minutes returned with Doctor R - . The two physicians conferred for some time, speaking in under tones. Mr. Dexter heard the words "congestion of the brain" and "brain fever," with increasing alarm.

"Well, doctors, how do you decide the case?" he inquired anxiously, as their conference terminated.

"There is a strong tendency to congestion of the brain," was replied by Doctor G -, "but, it is our opinion that we can check this tendency. Your wife, Mr. Dexter, is seriously ill. An experienced nurse must be had without delay. And every possible attention given, so as to second at all points the treatment under which she will be placed. A favorable result will doubtless crown our efforts. I present the case as a serious one, because it is so in its requirement of skill and unfailing attention."

The doctors did not err in their estimate of the case. The illness of Mrs. Dexter proved to be very serious. It was a brain fever. Four weeks elapsed before she was able to be removed from Newport to her home, and then she was so feeble in body and mind as to present but the shadowy semblance of her former self.

Very slowly did health flow back through her exhausted system. But a cheerful mind did not come with returning vigor. Her, spirit had bowed itself towards the earth; and power to rise again into the bracing atmosphere and warm sunshine, was not restored for a long period.

T.S. Arthur

CHAPTER XVI

AT Albany, Mr. Hendrickson found Miss Arden awaiting him. The warmth of her reception showed that he was more in her eyes than a pleasant friend. And in his regard she held the highest place - save one.

The meeting with Mrs. Dexter at Newport was unfortunate. Hendrickson had looked right down into her heart; reading a page, the writing on which she would have died rather than have revealed. Her pure regard for him was her own deeply hidden secret. It was a lamp burning in the sepulchre of buried hope. She could no more extinguish the sacred fire than quench her own existence.

But thrown suddenly off her guard, she had betrayed this secret to unlawful eyes. Hendrickson had read it. And she too had read his heart. After the lapse of more than a year they had met; and without wrong on either side had acknowledged a mutual inextinguishable love.

"You are not well, Mr. (sic) Henrickson." Many times, and with undisguised concern, was this said by Miss Arden, during the journey to Niagara.

"Only a slight headache;" or, "I'm well enough, but feel dull;" or, "The trip from Newport fatigued me," would be answered, and an effort made to be more companionable. But the task was difficult, and the position in which the young man found himself particularly embarrassing. His thoughts were not with

Miss Arden, but with Mrs. Dexter. Before the unexpected meeting at Newport, he had believed himself so far released from that entanglement of the heart, as to be free to make honorable advances to Miss Arden. But he saw his error now. With him marriage was something more than a good matrimonial arrangement, in which parties secure external advantages. To love Miss Arden better than any other living woman, he now saw to be impossible - and unless he could so love her, he dared not marry her. That was risking a great deal too much. His position became, therefore, an embarrassing one. Her brother was an old friend. They had been college companions. The sister he had known for some years, but had never been particularly interested in her until within a few months. Distancing his observation, her mind had matured; and the graces of art, education and accomplishment, had thrown their winning attractions around her. First, almost as a brother, he began to feel proud of her beauty and intelligence; admiration followed, and, before he was aware of the tendency of his feelings, they had taken on a warmer than fraternal glow.

All things tended to encourage this incipient regard; and, as Miss Arden herself favored it, and ever turned towards Hendrickson the sunniest side of her character, he found himself drawn onwards almost imperceptibly; and had even begun to think seriously of her as his wife, when the meeting with Mrs. Dexter revealed the existence of sentiments on both sides that gave the whole subject a new aspect.

A very difficult problem now presented itself to the mind of Mr. Hendrickson, involving questions of duty, questions of honor, and questions of feeling. It is not surprising that Miss Arden found a change in her travelling companion, nor that her visit to Niagara proved altogether unsatisfactory. No one could have been kindlier, more attentive, or more studious to make her visit attractive. But his careful avoidance of all compliments, and the absence of every thing lover-like, gave her heart the alarm. It was in vain that she put forth every chaste, womanly allurement; his eyes did not brighten, nor his cheeks glow, nor his tones become warmer. He was not to be

T.S. Arthur

driven from the citadel of his honor. A weaker, more selfish, and more external man, would have yielded. But Hendrickson, like the woman he had lost, was not made of "common clay," nor cast in any of humanity's ruder moulds. He was of purer essence and higher spiritual organization than the masses; and principle had now quite as much to do with his actions as feeling. He could be a martyr, but not a villain.

Two days were spent at Niagara, and then Hendrickson and Miss Arden returned, and went to Saratoga. It did not, of course, escape the notice of Hendrickson, that his manner to his travelling companion was effecting a steady change in her spirits; and he was not lacking in perception as to the cause. It revealed to him the sincerity of her regard; but added to the pain from which he was suffering, increasing it almost to the point where endurance fails.

It was a relief to Hendrickson when he was able to place Miss Arden under the care of her mother, who had remained at Saratoga. On the evening after his arrival, he was sitting alone in one of the drawing-rooms, when a lady crossed from the other side, and joined another lady near him.

"Mrs. De Lisle," said the latter, as she arose.

"Good evening, Mrs. Anthony!" and the ladies sat down together.

"I have just received a sad letter from Newport," said Mrs. De Lisle.

"Indeed! What has happened there?"

"Our sweet young friend is dangerously ill."

"Who? Mrs. Dexter?"

"Yes."

"Mrs. De Lisle! She was in perfect health, to all appearance, when she left here."

"So I thought. But she has suddenly been stricken down with a brain fever, and her physicians regard her condition as most critical."

"You distress me beyond measure!" said Mrs. Anthony.

"My friend writes that three physicians are in attendance; and that they report her case as dangerous in the extreme. I did not intend going there until next week, but, unless my husband strongly objects, I will leave to-morrow. Good nursing is quite as essential as medical skill."

"Go, by all means, if you can," replied Mrs. Anthony. "Dear child! I shouldn't wonder if that jealous husband of hers had done something to induce this attack. Brain fever don't come on without mental excitement of some kind. I can't bear him; and I believe, if the truth were known, it would be found that she hates the very sight of him. He's a man made of money; and that's saying the best that can be said. As to qualities of the mind and heart, she ranks, in everything, his superior. What a sacrifice of all that such a woman holds dear must have been made when she consented to become the wedded wife of Leon Dexter!"

Hendrickson heard no more, for a third party coming up at the moment, led to a change in the conversation. At the same instant Mrs. Arden and her daughter entered the room, and he arose and stepped forward to meet them.

"How pale you look, Mr. Hendrickson!" said Mrs. Arden, with concern. "Are you not well?"

"I have not felt as bright as usual, for some days," he answered, trying to force a smile, but without success. "Your daughter has, no doubt, already informed you that I proved myself one of the dullest of travelling companions."

"Oh, no," Miss Arden spoke up quickly. "Ma knows that I gave you credit for being exceedingly agreeable. But, indeed, Mr. Hendrickson, you look ill."

"I am slightly indisposed," he answered, "and with your leave will retire to my room. I shall feel better after lying down."

"Go by all means," said Mrs. Arden.

Hendrickson bowed low, and, passing them, left the parlor almost hurriedly.

"Dangerously ill! A brain fever!" he said aloud, as he gained his own apartment and shut the door behind him. He was deeply disturbed. That their unexpected meeting had something to do with this sudden sickness he now felt sure. Her strong, though quickly controlled agitation he had seen; it was a revelation never to be forgotten; and showed the existence of a state of feeling in regard to her husband which must render her very existence a burden. That she was closely watched, he had seen, as well as heard. And it did not appear to him improbable, considering the spirit he had observed her display, that coincident with his departure from Newport, some jealous accusations had been made, half maddening her spirit, and stunning her brain with excitement.

"Angel in the keeping of a fiend!" he exclaimed, as imagination drew improbable scenes of persecution. "How my heart aches for you - yearns towards you - longs for the dear privilege of making all your paths smooth and fragrant; all your hours golden-winged; all your states peaceful! How precious you are to me! Precious as my own soul - dear counterpart! loving complement! Vain, as your own strife with yourself, has been my strife. The burden has been too heavy for us; the ordeal too fiery. My brain grows wild at thought of this terrible wrong."

The image of Miss Arden flitted before him.

"Beautiful - loving - pure!" he said, "I might win you for my bride; but will not so wrong you as to offer a divided heart. All things forbid!"

Mr. Hendrickson did not leave his room that evening. At ten o'clock a servant knocked at his door. Mrs. Arden had sent her compliments, and desired to know if he were better than when he left her?

"Much better," he answered; and the servant departed.

Midnight found him still in strife with himself. Now he walked the floor in visible agitation; and now sat motionless, with head bowed, and arms folded across his bosom. The impression of sleep was far from his overwrought brain. One thing he decided, and that was to leave Saratoga by the earliest morning train, and go with all possible haste to Newport. Suspense in regard to Mrs. Dexter he felt it would be impossible for him to bear.

"But what right have you to take all this interest in a woman who is another's lawful wife?" he asked, in the effort to stem the tide of his feelings.

"I will not stop to debate questions of right," so he answered within his own thoughts. "She *is* the wife of another, and I would die rather than stain her pure escutcheon with a thought of dishonor. I cease to love her when I imagine her capable of being false, in even the smallest act, to her marriage vows. But the right to love, Heaven gave me when my soul was created to make one with hers. I will keep myself pure that I may remain worthy of her."

On the evening of the next day Hendrickson arrived at Newport. Almost the first man he encountered was Dexter.

"How is Mrs. Dexter?" he asked, forgetting in his anxiety and suspense the relation he bore to this man. His eager inquiry met a cold response accompanied by a scowl.

"I am not aware that you have any particular interest in Mrs. Dexter!"

And the angry husband turned from him abruptly.

"How unfortunate!" Hendrickson said to himself as he passed.

At the office he put the same inquiry.

"Very ill," was the answer.

"Is she thought to be dangerous?"

"I believe so."

Beyond this he gained no further intelligence from the clerk. A little while afterwards he saw Mrs. Florence in one of the parlors, and joined her immediately. From her he learned that Mrs. Dexter remained wholly unconscious, but that the physicians regarded her symptoms as favorable.

"Do they think her out of danger?" he asked, with more interest in his manner than he wished to betray.

"Yes."

He could scarcely withhold an exclamation.

"What do you think, madam?" he inquired.

"I cannot see deeper than a physician," she answered. "But my observation does not in anything gainsay the opinion which has been expressed. I am encouraged to hope for recovery."

"Do you remain here any time?"

"I shall not leave until I see Mrs. Dexter on the safe side and in good hands," was replied.

"Have you heard any reason assigned for this fearful attack?" inquired Hendrickson.

Mrs. Florence shook her head.

Not caring to manifest an interest in Mrs. Dexter that might attract attention, or occasion comment, Hendrickson dropped the subject. During the evening he threw himself in the way of the physician, and gathered all he desired to know from him. The report was so favorable that he determined to leave Newport by the midnight boat for New York and return home, which he accordingly did.

CHAPTER XVII

THE season at Newport closed, and the summer birds of fashion flitted away. But Mrs. Dexter still remained, and in a feeble condition. It was as late as November before the physician in attendance would consent to her removal. She was then taken home, but so changed that even her nearest friends failed to recognize in her wan, sad, dreary face, anything of its old expression.

No man could have been kinder - no man could have lavished warmer attentions on another than were lavished on his wife by Mr. Dexter. With love-like assiduity, he sought to awaken her feelings to some interest in life; not tiring, though she remained as coldly passive as marble. But she gave him back no sign. There was neither self-will, perverseness, nor antagonism, in this; but paralysis instead. Emotion had died.

It was Christmas before Mrs. Dexter left her room - and then she was so weak as to need a supporting arm. Tonics only were administered by her physician; but if they acted at all, it was so feebly that scarcely any good result appeared. The cause of weakness lay far beyond the reach of his medicines.

With the slow return of bodily strength and mental activity, was developed in the mind of Mrs. Dexter a feeling of repugnance to her husband that went on increasing. She did not struggle against this feeling, because she knew, by instinct, that all resistance would be vain. It was something over which she could not possibly have control; the stern protest of nature against an alliance unblessed by love.

One day, during mid-winter, her best friend, Mrs. De Lisle, in making one of her usual visits, found her sitting alone, and in tears. It was the first sign of struggling emotion that she had yet seen, and she gladly recognized the tokens of returning life.

"Showers for the heart," she said, almost smiling, as she kissed the pale invalid. "May the green grass and the sweet smiling violets soon appear."

Mrs. Dexter did not reply, but with unusual signs of feeling, hid her face in the garments of her friend.

"How are you to-day?" asked Mrs. De Lisle, after she had given time for emotion to subside.

"About as usual," was answered, and Mrs. Dexter looked with regaining calmness into her face.

"I have not seen you so disturbed for weeks," said Mrs. De Lisle.

"I have not felt so wild a strife in my soul for months," was answered. "Oh, that I could die! It was this prayer that unlocked the long closed fountain of tears."

"With God are the issues of life," said Mrs. De Lisle. "We must each of us wait His good time - patiently, hopefully, self-denyingly wait."

"I know! I know!" replied Mrs. Dexter. "But I cannot look along the way that lies before me without a shudder. The path is too difficult."

"You will surely receive strength."

"I would rather die!" A slight convulsion ran through her frame.

"Don't look into the future, dear young friend! Only to-day's duties are required; and strength ever comes with the duty."

"Not even God can give strength for mine," said Mrs. Dexter, almost wildly.

"Hush! hush! the thought is impious!" Mrs. De Lisle spoke in warning tones.

"Not impious, but true. God did not lay these heavy burdens on me. My own hands placed them there. If I drag a pillar down upon myself, will God make my bones iron so that they shall not be broken? No, Mrs. De Lisle; there is only one hope for me, and that is in death; and I pray for it daily."

"You state the case too strongly," said Mrs. De Lisle. "God prevides as well as provides. His providence determining what is best for us; and His previdence counteracts our ignorance, self-will, or evil purposes, and saves us from the destruction we would blindly meet. He never permits any act in His creatures, for which He does not previde an agency that turns the evil that would follow into good. Your case is parallel to thousands. As a free woman, you took this most important step. God could not have prevented it without destroying that freedom which (sic) constitues your individuality, and makes you a recipient of life from Him. But He can sustain you in the duties and trials you have assumed; and He will do it, if you permit Him to substitute His divine strength for your human weakness. In all trial, affliction, calamity, suffering, there is a germ of angelic life. It is through much tribulation that the Kingdom of Heaven is gained. Some spirits require intenser fires for purification than others; and yours may be of this genus. God is the refiner and the purifier; and He will not suffer any of the gold and silver to be lost. Dear friend! do not shrink away from the ordeal."

"I am not strong enough yet." It was all the reply Mrs. Dexter made. Her voice was mournful in the extreme.

"Wait for strength. As your day is, so shall it be."

Mrs. Dexter shook her head.

"What more can I say?" Mrs. De Lisle spoke almost sadly, for she could not see that her earnestly spoken counsel had wrought any good effect.

"Nothing! nothing! dear friend!" answered Mrs. Dexter, still very mournfully.

A little while she was silent; and seemed in debate with herself. At length she said -

"Dear Mrs. De Lisle! To you I have unveiled my heart more than to any other human being. And I am constrained to draw the veil a little farther aside. To speak will give relief; and as you are wiser, help may come. At Saratoga, I confided to you something on that most delicate of all subjects, my feelings towards my husband. I have yet more to say! Shall I go farther in these painful, almost forbidden revelations?"

"Say on," was the answer, "I shall listen with no vain curiosity."

"I am conscious," Mrs. Dexter began, "of a new feeling towards my husband. I call it new, for, if only the fuller development of an old impression, it has all the vividness of a new-born emotion. Before my illness, I saw many things in him to which I could attach myself; and I was successful, in a great measure, in depressing what was repellant, and in magnifying the attractive. But now I seem to have been gifted with a faculty of sight that enables me to look through the surface as if it were only transparent glass; and I see qualities, dispositions, affections, and tendencies, against which all my soul revolts. I do not say that they are evil; but they are all of the earth earthy. Nor do I claim to be purer and better than he is - only so different, that I prefer death to union. It is in vain to struggle against my feelings, and I have ceased to struggle."

"You are still weak in body and mind," answered Mrs. De Lisle. "All the pulses of returning life are feeble. Do not attempt this struggle now."

"It must be now, or never," was returned. "The current is bearing me away. A little while, and the most agonizing strife with wave and tempest will prove of no avail."

"Look aloft, dear friend! Look aloft!" said Mrs. De Lisle. "Do not listen to the maddening dash of waters below, nor gaze at the shuddering bark; but upwards, upwards, through cloud-rifts, into heaven!"

"I have tried to look upwards - I *have* looked upwards - but the sight of heaven only makes earth more terrible by contrast."

"Who have washed their robes and made them white in the blood of the Lamb?" asked Mrs. De Lisle, in a deep, earnest voice. A pause, and then - "They who have come up through great tribulation! Think of this, dear friend. Heaven may be beautiful in your eyes, but the way to heaven is by earthly paths. You cannot get there, except by the way of duty; and your duty is not to turn away from, but to your husband, in the fulfillment of your marriage vows - to the letter. I say nothing of the spirit, but the letter of this law you must keep. Mr. Dexter is not an evil-minded man. He is a good citizen, and desires to be a good husband. His life, to the world, is irreproachable. The want of harmony in taste, feeling and character, is no reason for disseverance. You cannot leave him, and be guiltless in the eyes of God or man."

"I did not speak of leaving him," said Mrs. Dexter, looking up strangely into the face of Mrs. De Lisle.

"But you have thought of it," was answered. A flush dyed the pale face of Mrs. Dexter. "Oh, my friend, beware of evil counsellors! Mrs. Anthony" -

"Has never looked into my heart. It is shut and fastened with clasps of iron when she is near," returned Mrs. Dexter.

"The presence of such a woman suggests rebellion," said Mrs. De Lisle; "her thoughts are communicated by another way than speech. Is it not so?"

"Perhaps it is. I feel the spirit of antagonism rising whenever I am with her. I grow restive - impatient of these bonds - indignant towards my husband; though the subject is never mentioned."

"Be on your guard against her, my young friend. Her principles are not religiously sound. This I say to you, because duty requires me to say it. Placed in your position, and with your feelings towards her husband, if no personal and selfish consideration came in to restrain her, she would not hesitate at separation - nay, I fear, not even at a guilty compact with another."

"You shock me!" said Mrs. Dexter.

"I speak to you my real sentiments; and in warning. In your present state of mind, be very reserved towards her. You are not strong enough to meet her quick intelligence, nor able to guard yourself against her subtle insinuations. When was she here last?"

A sudden thought prompted the question.

"She left just before you came in," answered Mrs. Dexter.

"And your mind has been disturbed, not tranquillized, by her visit?"

"I am disturbed, as you see."

"On what subject did she speak?" asked Mrs. De Lisle.

"You know her usual theme?"

T.S. Arthur

"Inharmonious marriages?"

"Yes."

"I do not wonder that you were disturbed. How could it be otherwise?"

"She gives utterance to many truths," said Mrs. Dexter.

"But even truth may be so spoken as to have all the evil effect of error," was promptly answered.

"Can truth ever do harm? Is it not the mind's light? Truth shows us the way in which we may walk safely," said Mrs. Dexter, with some earnestness of manner.

"Light, by which the eye sees, will become a minister of destruction, if the eye is inflamed. A mind diseased cannot bear strong gleams of truth. They will blind and deceive, rather than illustrate. The rays must be softened. Of the many truths to which Mrs. Anthony gave utterance this morning, which most affected your mind?"

"She spoke," said Mrs. Dexter, after a little reflection, "of natural affinities and repulsions, which take on sometimes the extreme condition of idiosyncrasies. Of conjunctions of soul in true marriages, and of disjunction and disgust where no true marriage exists."

"Did she explain what she understood by a true marriage?" asked Mrs. De Lisle.

"I do not remember any formal explanation. But her meaning was obvious."

"What, then, did she mean?"

A little while Mrs. Dexter thought, and then answered -

"She thinks that men and women are born partners, and that only they who are fortunate enough to meet are ever happy in marriage - are, in fact, really married."

"How is a woman to know that she is rightly mated?" asked Mrs. De Lisle.

"By the law of affinities. The instincts of our nature are never at fault."

"So the thief who steals your watch will say the instincts of his nature all prompted to the act. If our lives were orderly as in the beginning, Mrs. Dexter, we might safely follow the soul's unerring instincts. But, unfortunately, this is not the case; and instinct needs the law of revelation and the law of reason for its guide."

"You believe in true, interior marriages?" said Mrs. Dexter.

"Yes, marriages for eternity."

"And that they are made here?"

Mrs. De Lisle did not answer immediately.

"The preparation for eternal marriage is here," she said, speaking thoughtfully.

Mrs. Dexter looked at her like one in doubt as to the meaning of what she heard. She then said:

"In a true marriage, souls must conjoin by virtue of an original affinity. In a word, the male and the female must be born for each other."

"There are a great many vague notions afloat on this subject," said Mrs. De Lisle; "and a great deal of flippant talk. If there are men and women born for each other, one thing is very certain, both need a great deal of alteration before they can unite perfectly; and the trial will, in most cases, not so fully prove this theory of quality in sexual creation as you might suppose. 'Behold, I was shapen in iniquity!' If this were not true of every one, there might be a little more hope for happiness in marriage. Let us imagine the union of two persons, born with that original containing affinity of which you speak - and the existence of which I do not deny. We will suppose that the man inherits from his ancestors certain evil and selfish qualities; and that the woman inherits from her ancestors certain evil and selfish qualities also. They marry young, and before either is disciplined by right principle, or regenerated by Divine truth. Now, this being the case, do you suppose that, in the beginning, their pulses will beat in perfect harmony? That there will be no jarring in the machinery of their lives?"

Mrs. De Lisle paused, but received no answer.

"In just the degree," she continued, "that each is selfish, and fails to repress that selfishness, will the other suffer pain or feel repulsion? And they will not come into the true accordance of their lives until both are purified through a denial of self, and an elevation of the spiritual above the natural. For it is in the spiritual plane where true marriages take place; and only with those who are regenerated. All that goes before is preparation."

Mrs. Dexter continued looking earnestly into the face of Mrs. De Lisle.

"Does your thought follow me?" asked the latter.

"Yes," was all the answer.

"If true marriages are for eternity, each of the partners must be born into spiritual life; and that birth is always with pain. The husband, instead of being a mere natural and selfish man, must be a lover of higher and purer things. He must be a seeker after Divine intelligence, that he may be lifted with wisdom coming from the infinite Source of wisdom. And the wife, elevating her affections through self-denial and repression of the natural, must acquire a love for the spiritual wisdom of her husband before her soul can make one with his. Do you comprehend this?"

"Dimly. He must be wise in heavenly love; and she a lover of heavenly wisdom."

"There must be something more," said Mrs. De Lisle.

"What more?"

"No two masculine souls are alike, and heavenly wisdom is infinite. The finite mind receives only a portion of the Divine intelligence. Each, therefore, is in the love of growing wise in a certain degree or direction. The feminine soul, to make conjunction perfect, must be a lover of wisdom in that degree, or direction."

"You bewilder me," said Mrs. Dexter.

"Let me rather enlighten. The great truth I wish to make clear to you is that there can be no marriage in the higher sense without spiritual regeneration. By nature we are evil - that is selfish; for self love is the very essence of all evil - and until heavenly life is born in us there can be no interior marriage conjunction. It is possible, then - and I want you to look the proposition fairly in the face - for two who are created for each other, to live very unhappily together during the first years of their married life. Do you ask why? Because both are selfish by nature; and self seeks its own delight. I have sometimes thought," continued Mrs. De Lisle, "in pondering this subject, that those who are born for each other are not often permitted to struggle together in painful antagonism during the stern ordeals through which so many have to pass ere self is subdued, and the fires of Divine love kindled on the heart's altars."

"Meeting life's discipline apart, or in strife with an alien," said

Mrs. Dexter.

"As you will. But the lesson, I trust, is clear. Only they who bear the cross can wear the crown. The robes must be made white in the blood of the Lamb. And now, dear friend! if you would be worthy of an eternal marriage, take up your cross. If there is a noble, manly soul to which you would be conjoined forever, set earnestly about the task of preparation for that union. The wedding garment must be wrought; the lamps trimmed and burning. Not in neglect of duty; not in weak repinings, or helpless despondency is this work done; but in daily duty. The soul of your husband is precious in the eyes of God as your own. Never forget this. And it may be a part of your heaven-assigned work - nay, is - to help him to rise into a higher life. May you grow angel-minded in the good work!"

"How tranquil I have become," said Mrs. Dexter, a little while afterwards. "The heavy pressure on heart and brain is removed."

"You have not been thinking of yourself; and that has brought a change in your state of feeling. Cease to struggle in your bonds; but rise up and go forward with brave heart, and be true as steel to all your obligations. The way may look dark, the burdens heavy; but fear not. Move on, and Divine light will fall upon your path; stoop to the burden, and Divine strength will be given. So I counsel you, dear sister! And I pray you heed the counsel."

CHAPTER XVIII

ON the day after the interview with Mrs. De Lisle, Mrs. Dexter, whose mind had been lifted quite above its morbid state, was sitting alone at one of the parlor windows. She had been noting, with curious interest, the types of character in faces that met her eyes, and then disappeared to give place to others as singularly varied, when a new countenance, on which her eyes fell, lighted up suddenly. It was that of Hendrickson, whom she had not seen since their parting at Newport. He paused, lifted his hat, bowed and went on. It was no cold, formal recognition; but one full of earnest life, and warm with sudden feeling. Mrs. Dexter was conscious of a quick heart-throb that sent a glow to her pale cheeks.

Unfortunate coincidence! The next face, presenting itself almost in the same instant of time, was that of her husband. It was full two hours earlier than the period of his usual return home.

He had seen the expression of Hendrickson's countenance; and also the responsive change in that of his wife. At once it occurred to him that an understanding had been established between him and Mrs. Dexter, and that this was the beginning of a series of interviews, to be carried on during his absence. Mr. Dexter was an impulsive man. Without giving himself time for reflection, he strode into the parlor, and said with a cutting sneer -

"You have your own entertainments, I see, in your husband's

absence. But" - and his manner grew stern, while his tones were threatening, "you must not forget that we are in America and not Paris; and that I am an American, and not a French husband. You are going a step too far, madam!"

Too much confounded for speech, Mrs. Dexter, into whose face the blood had rushed, dying it to a deep crimson, sat looking at her husband, an image, in his eyes, of guilt confessed.

"I warn you," he added, "not to presume on me in this direction! And I further warn you, that if I ever catch that scoundrel in my house, or in your company, I will shoot him down like a dog!"

Mrs. Dexter was too feeble for a shock like this. The crimson left her face. While her husband yet glared angrily upon her, a deathly hue overspread her features, and she fainted, falling forward upon the floor. He sprung to catch her in his arms, but it was too late. She struck with a heavy concussion, against temple and cheek, bruising them severely.

When Mrs. Dexter recovered, she was in her own room lying upon her bed. No one was there but her husband. He looked grave to sadness. She looked at him a single moment, then shut her eyes and turned her face away. Mr. Dexter neither moved nor spoke. A more wretched man was scarcely in existence. He believed all against his wife that his words expressed; yet was he conscious of unpardonable indiscretion - and he was deeply troubled as to the consequences of his act. Mrs. Dexter was fully restored to consciousness, and remembered distinctly, the blasting intimations of her husband. But, she was wholly free from excitement, and was thinking calmly.

"Will you send for my aunt?" Mrs. Dexter turned her face from the wall as she said this, speaking in a low but firm voice.

"Not now. Why do you wish to see her?" Mr. Dexter's tones

were low and firm also.

"I shall return to her," said Mrs. Dexter.

"What do you mean?" Feeling betrayed itself.

"As I am a degraded being in your eyes, you do not, of course, wish me to remain under your roof. And, as you have degraded me by foul and false accusations, against the bare imagination of which my soul revolts, I can no longer share your home, nor eat the bread which your hand provides for me. Where there is no love on one side and no faith on the other, separation becomes inevitable."

"You talk madly," said Mr. Dexter.

"Not madly, but soberly," she answered. "There is an unpardonable sin against a virtuous wife, and you have committed it. Forgiveness is impossible. I wish to see my aunt. Will you send for her, Mr. Dexter?"

"It was a dark day for me, Jessie, when I first looked upon your face," said Mr. Dexter.

"And darker still for me, sir. Yet, after my constrained marriage, I tried, to the best of my ability, to be all you desired. That I failed, was no fault of mine."

"Nor mine," was answered.

"Let us not make matters worse by crimination and recrimination," said Mrs. Dexter. "It will take nothing from our future peace to remember that we parted in forbearance, instead of with passionate accusation."

"You are surely beside yourself, Jessie!" exclaimed Mr. Dexter.

She turned her face away, and made no response.

Dexter was frightened. "Could it be possible," he asked himself, "that his wife really purposed a separation?" The fact loomed up before his imagination with all of its appalling consequences.

A full half hour passed, without a word more from the lips of either. Then Mr. Dexter quietly retired from the room. He had no sooner done this, than Mrs. Dexter arose from the bed, and commenced making changes in her dress. Her face was very white, and her movements unsteady, like the movements of a person just arisen from an exhausting sickness. There was some appearance of hurry and agitation in her manner.

About an hour later, and just as twilight had given place to darkness, Mrs. Loring who was sitting with her daughters, lifted her eyes from the work in her hands, and leaned her head in a listening attitude. The door bell had rung, and a servant was moving along the passage. A moment of suspense, and then light steps were heard and the rustling of a woman's garments.

"Jessie!" exclaimed Mrs. Loring, as Mrs. Dexter entered the sitting-room." She was enveloped in a warm cloak, with a hood drawn over her head. As she pushed the latter from her partly hidden face, her aunt saw a wildness about her eyes, that suggested, in connection with this unheralded visit of the feeble invalid, the idea of mental derangement. Starting forward, and almost encircling her with her arms, she said -

"My dear child! what is the meaning of this visit? Where is Mr. Dexter? Did he come with you?"

"I am cold," she answered, with a shiver. "The air is piercing." And she turned towards the grate, spreading her hands to the genial warmth.

"Did Mr. Dexter come with you?" Mrs. Loring repeated the question.

"No; I came alone," was the quietly spoken answer.

"You did not walk?"

"Yes."

"Why, Jessie! You imprudent child! Does Mr. Dexter know of this?"

There was no reply to this question.

"Aunt Phoebe," said Mrs. Dexter, turning from the fire, "can I see you alone?"

"Certainly, dear," and placing an arm around her, Mrs. Loring went with her niece from the room.

"You have frightened me, child," said the aunt, as soon as they were alone. "What has happened? Why have you come at this untimely hour, and with such an imprudent exposure of your health?"

"*I have come home, Aunt Phoebe!*" Mrs. Dexter stood and looked steadily into the face of her aunt.

"Home, Jessie?" Mrs. Loring was bewildered.

"I have no other home in the wide world, Aunt Phoebe." The sadness of Jessie's low, steady voice, went deep down into the worldly heart of Mrs. Loring.

"Child! child! What *do* you mean?" exclaimed the astonished woman.

"Simply, that I have come back to you again - to die, I trust, and that right early!"

"Where is Mr. Dexter? What has happened? Oh, Jessie! Speak plainly!" said Mrs. Loring, much agitated.

"I have left Mr. Dexter, Aunt Phoebe." She yet spoke in a calm voice. "And shall not return to him. If you will let me have that little chamber again, which I used to call my own, I will bless you for the sanctuary, and hide myself in it from the world. I do not think I shall burden you a long time, Aunt Phoebe. I am passing through conflicts and enduring pains that are too severe for me. Feeble nature is fast giving way. The time will not be long, dear aunt!"

"Sit down, child! There! Sit down." And Mrs. Loring led her niece to a chair. "This is a serious business, Jessie," she added, in a troubled voice. "I am bewildered by your strange language. What does it mean? Speak to me plainly. I am afraid you are dreaming."

"I wish it were a dream, aunt. But no - all is fearfully real. For causes of which I cannot now speak, I have separated myself from Mr. Dexter, and shall never live with him again. Our ways have parted, and forever."

"Jessie! Jessie! What madness! Are you beside yourself? Is this a step to be taken without a word of consultation with friends?"

Mrs. Loring, as soon as her mind began clearly to comprehend what her niece had done, grew strongly excited. Mrs. Dexter did not reply, but let her eyes fall to the floor, and remained silent. She had no defence to make at any human tribunal.

"Why have you done this, Jessie?" demanded her aunt.

"Forgive my reply, Aunt Phoebe; I can make no other now. *The reason is with God and my own heart.* He can look deeper than any human eyes have power to see; and comprehend more than I can put in words. My cause is with Him. If my burdens are too heavy, He will not turn from me because I fall fainting by the way."

"Jessie, what is the meaning of this?" Mrs. Loring spoke in a suddenly changed voice, and coming close to her niece, looked earnestly into her face. "Here is a bad bruise on your right cheek, and another on the temple just above. And the skin is inflamed around the edges of these bruises, showing them to be recent. How came this, Jessie?"

"Bruises? Are you certain?"

"Why, yes, child! and bad ones, too."

Mrs. Dexter looked surprised. She raised her hand to her cheek and temple, and pressing slightly, was conscious of pain.

"I believe I fainted in the parlor this afternoon," she said; "I must have fallen to the floor."

"Fainted! From what cause?" asked Mrs. Loring.

Mrs. Dexter was silent.

"Was it from sudden illness?"

"Yes."

Mrs. Loring was not satisfied with this brief answer. Imagination suggested some personal outrage.

"Was Mr. Dexter in the parlor when you fainted?" she asked.

"Yes."

"Why did he not save you from falling?"

"I am very cold, aunt; and my head turns. Let me lie down." Mrs. Dexter made an effort to rise. As Mrs. Loring caught her arms, she felt them shiver. Quickly leading her to the bed, she laid her in among the warm blankets; but external warmth could not subdue the nervous chill that shook her frame in every part.

T.S. Arthur

"The doctor must be sent for," said Mrs. Loring - and she was about leaving the bedside.

"No, no, aunt!" Mrs. Dexter caught her hand, and held her back. "I want no physician - only quiet and seclusion. Have my own little room prepared for me, and let me go there to-night."

Mrs. Loring sat down undecided, and in great perplexity of mind.

"Listen!" Some one had rung the door-bell violently.

"Aunt!" Mrs. Dexter started up and laid her hand on the arm of Mrs. Loring. "If that is Mr. Dexter, remember that I positively refuse to meet him. I am ill, as you can see; and I warn you that the agitation of a forced interview may cost me my life."

"If it is Mr. Dexter, what shall I say? Hark! Yes! It is his step, and his voice."

"Say that I cannot be seen, and that I have left him forever."

"But, Jessie" -

"Aunt Loring, remonstrance is vain! I have not taken this step without a deep consciousness of being right; and no power on earth can lead me to retrace it. Let him comprehend that, in its plain significance; the sooner he does so the better will it be for both."

"Mr. Dexter wishes to see you," said a servant, coming to the door.

"Say that I will be down in a moment."

Mrs. Loring stood for some time, endeavoring to collect her thoughts and calm her feelings. She then went down to the parlor.

CHAPTER XIX

"Is Jessie here?" inquired Mr. Dexter, in a hurried manner.

"She is," replied Mrs. Loring.

"I wish to see her."

"Sit down, Mr. Dexter. I want to speak with you about Jessie."

Mr. Dexter sat down, though with signs of impatience.

"What is the meaning of this? What has happened, Mr. Dexter?"

"Only a slight misunderstanding. Jessie is over sensitive. But I must see her immediately; and alone, if you please, Mrs. Loring."

"I am sorry, Mr. Dexter, but Jessie will not see you."

"Not see me!"

"No, Sir."

"Go and say that I am here, and that I must see her, if only for a single moment."

"She knows you are here, Mr. Dexter; and her message is - 'Say that I cannot seen.'"

"Where is she?" Mr. Dexter moved towards the door; but Mrs. Loring, who had taken it into her head that personal abuse - a blow, perhaps - was the cause of Jessie's flight from the residence of her husband - (she could understand and be properly indignant at such an outrage), stepping before him said -

"Don't forget, sir, that this is my house! You cannot pass into any of its apartments unless I give permission. And such permission is now withheld. My niece is in no condition for exciting interviews. There has been enough of that for one day, I should think."

"What do you mean? What has she said?" demanded Mr. Dexter, looking almost fiercely at Mrs. Loring.

"Nothing!" was replied. "She refuses to answer my questions. But I see that her mind is greatly agitated, while her person bears evidence of cruel treatment."

"Mrs. Loring!" Dexter understood her meaning, and instantly grew calm. "Evidences of cruel treatment!"

"Yes, sir! Her cheek and temple are discolored from a recent bruise. How came this?"

"She fainted, and struck herself in falling."

"In your presence?"

"Yes."

"And you did not put forth a hand to save her!"

Mrs. Loring's foregone conclusions were running away with her.

"Excuse me madam," said Mr. Dexter, coldly, "you are going beyond the record. I am not here at the confessional, but to see my wife. Pray, do do not interpose needless obstacles."

There was enough of contempt in the tones of Mr. Dexter to wound the pride and fire the self-love of Mrs. Loring; and enough of angry excitement about him, to give her a new impression of his character.

"You cannot see Jessie to-night," she answered firmly. "She has flown back to me in wild affright - the mere wreck of what she was, poor child! when I gave her into your keeping - and the inviolable sanctity of my house is around her. I much fear, Leon Dexter, that you have proved recreant to your trust - that you have not loved, protected, and cherished that delicate flower. The sweetness of her life is gone?"

The woman of the world had (sic) actally warmed into sentiment.

"It is I who have suffered wrong," said Mr. Dexter. "Sit down, Mrs. Loring, and hear me. If I cannot see my wife - if she willfully persists in the step she has taken - then will I clear my skirts. You, at least, if not the world, must know the truth. Sit down, madam, and listen."

They moved back from the door, and crossing the parlor, sat down together on a sofa.

"What is wrong?" asked Mrs. Loring, the manner and words of Mr. Dexter filling her mind with vague fear.

"Much," was answered.

"Say on."

"Your niece, I have reason to believe, is not true to me," said Dexter.

"Sir!" Astonishment and indignation blended in the tone of Mrs. Loring's voice.

T.S. Arthur

"I happened to come upon her unawares to-day, taking her in the very act of encouraging the attentions of a man whose presence and detected intimacy with her, at Newport, were the causes of her illness there."

"It is false!"

Both Dexter and Mrs. Loring started to their feet.

There stood Jessie, just within the door at the lower end of the parlor, her cheeks flushed, and her eyes bright with indignation.

"It is false, sir!" she repeated, in strong, clear tones.

Mr. Dexter, after the first moment of bewildering surprise, advanced towards his wife.

"It is false - false as the evil spirit who suggested a thought of your wife's dishonor!"

Saying this, Mrs. Dexter turned and glided away. Her husband made a motion to follow, but Mrs. Loring laid her hand upon his arm.

"Light breaks into my mind," she said. "It was because you charged her with dishonorable intent that she fled from you? A man should be well fortified with proofs before he ventures so far. I will believe nothing against her, except on the clearest evidence. Can you adduce it?"

There was a homely force in this mode of presenting the subject that had the effect to open the eyes of Dexter a little to the unpleasant aspect of his position. What proof had he of his wife's infidelity - and yet he had gone so far as to say that he had reason to believe her not true to him, and that she had been detected in questionable intimacy with some one at Newport!

"Can you adduce the evidence, Mr. Dexter?" repeated Mrs. Loring.

"I may have been hasty," he said, moving back into the room. "My words may have signified too much. But she has been imprudent."

"It is not true, sir!"

The voice of Jessie startled them again. She stood almost on the spot from which they had turned a moment before.

"It is not true, sir!" she repeated her words. "Not true, in any degree! All is but the ghost of a jealous fancy! And now, sir, beware how you attempt to connect my name with evil reports or surmises! I may be stung into demanding of you the proof, and in another place than this! Never, even in thought, have I dishonored you. That is a lower deep into which my nature can never fall; and you should have known me well enough to have had faith. Alas that it was not so!"

She passed from her husband's presence again, seeming almost to vanish where she stood.

"What is to be done?" said Mr. Dexter, turning towards Mrs. Loring, with a certain shame-facedness, that showed his own perception of the aspect in which his hasty conduct had placed him.

"It is impossible to answer that question now," replied Mrs. Loring. "These muddy waters must have time to run clear. As for Jessie, it is plain that she needs seclusion, and freedom from all causes of excitement. That you have wronged her deeply by your suspicions, I have not the shadow of a doubt - how deeply, conceding her innocence, you can say better than I."

"You will not encourage her in maintaining towards me her present attitude, Mrs. Loring?"

"Not if I see any hope of reconciliation. But I must know more of your lives during the past few months. I fear that you have wholly misunderstood your wife, and so alienated her that oblivion of the past is hopeless."

"Think of the exposure and disgrace," said Mr. Dexter.

"I do think of it; and the thought sickens me."

"You will surely advise her to return."

"I can promise nothing sir. Wait - wait - wait. I have no other advice to offer. My poor child has passed through fearful trials - that is plain; and she must have time for body and mind to recover themselves. Oh, sir! how could you, knowing her feeble condition, bear down upon her so heavily as you did this day. Your words must have fallen like heavy blows; for it seems that they struck her down senseless. A second attack of brain fever, should it unfortunately follow this agitation, will certainly prove fatal."

Dexter was silent.

"We must keep our own counsel for the present," he said, at length. "The public should know nothing of all this."

"In that we are agreed," answered Mrs. Loring. "My advice to you is, to leave Jessie, for the time being at least, to her own will. Serious prostration of all her faculties, I cannot but fear as a consequence. To-morrow, she will in all probability need her physician's care."

"How will you account for her condition, should his attendance be deemed necessary?"

Mrs. Loring shook her head.

"Events," she answered, "are too recent, and my mind too much bewildered to say what course I may deem it the wisest policy to pursue. I must await the occasion, and govern myself accordingly."

"Be very prudent, madam," said Mr. Dexter. "A single error may wreck everything."

"Her reputation is as dear to me as my own," replied Mrs. Loring, "and you may be very sure, that I will guard it as a most precious thing. The warning as to circumspection I pass to you."

Mr. Dexter made a movement to retire.

"I will see you in the morning," he said, "and in the meantime, account for Jessie's absence, by saying that she paid you a visit, going out imprudently, and found herself too much indisposed to return."

Mrs. Loring merely inclined her head. A little while Dexter stood looking at her, embarrassment and trouble written on every feature. Then bowing coldly, he retired.

T.S. Arthur

CHAPTER XX

WHEN Mrs. Loring went back to her chamber, after Mr. Dexter withdrew from the house, she found Jessie in bed, lying as still as if asleep. She looked up when her aunt came to the bedside - at first with stealthy, half-timid glances - then with more of trust, that changed into loving confidence. Mrs. Loring bent down and kissed her.

"Oh, Aunt Phoebe! that was very cruel in him."

"What was cruel, dear?"

The thoughts of Mrs. Loring went farther back than to the interview in her parlor.

"He tried to ruin me even in your regard."

"But he failed, Jessie. I will not believe the lowest whisper of an evil report against you."

"I am as pure in thought and as true in purpose, Aunt Phoebe, as when I went out from you. I do not love Mr. Dexter - I never loved him. Still that is no crime - only a necessity. He understood this in the beginning, and took the risk of happiness - so did I. But he was not satisfied with all that I could give. He wanted a heart, as well as a hand - a living, loving spirit, as well as a body. These he could not possess in me - for the heart loves not by compulsion. Then jealousy was born in his soul, and suspicion followed. Both were groundless. I felt a degrading sense of wrong; and at times, a spirit of rebellion. But I never gave place to a wandering thought - never gave occasion for wrong construction of my conduct. Ah, Aunt Phoebe! that marriage was a sad mistake. A union unblessed by love, is the commencement of a wretched life. It is the old story; and never loses its tragic interest. It was folly in the beginning, and it is madness now."

Mrs. Loring would have questioned her niece closely as to the meaning of Mr. Dexter's allusion to a certain individual as having been too intimate with his wife, but these closing remarks fell like rebuke upon her ears. She remembered how almost like a victim-lamb, Jessie had been led up to the marriage altar; and how she had overruled all objections, and appealing to her honor, had almost constrained her into the fulfillment of a promise that should never have been extorted. And so she remained silent.

"I knew it must come to this sooner or later," Jessie went on; "I knew that a time must arrive when the only alternative for me would be death or separation. The separation has taken place sooner than I had dared to hope; and for the act, I do not hold myself responsible. He flung me off! To a spirit like mine, his language was a strong repulsion; and I swept away from him with a force it would have been vain to resist. We are apart now, and apart forever."

"You are too much excited, Jessie," said Mrs. Loring, laying her finger upon the lips of her niece, "and I must enjoin silence and rest. I have faith in you. I will be your friend, though all the world pass coldly on in scorn."

Tears glistened in the eyes of Mrs. Dexter as she lifted them, with a thankful expression, to the face of her aunt, from whom she had not dared to hope for so tender a reception. She knew Mrs. Loring to be worldly-minded; she knew her to be a woman of not over delicate feelings; and as one easily affected by appearances. That she would blame, denounce, threaten, she had no doubt. A thought of approval, sympathy, aid or

T.S. Arthur

comfort in this fearful trial had not stirred in her imagination. This unlooked for kindness on the part of her aunt touched her deeply.

The fact was, Mr. Dexter had gone a step too far. The grossness of this outrage upon his wife, Mrs. Loring could appreciate, and it was just of the kind to arouse all her womanly indignation. A more refined act of cruelty she would not have understood; and might have adjudged her niece as capricious.

"Thank you, dear Aunt Phoebe, for this love and kindness!" Jessie could not help saying. "I need it; and, for all I have been as a wife, am worthy to receive it. As pure in thought and act as when I parted from you do I return; and now all I ask is to become again the occupant of that little chamber I once called my own; there to hide myself from all eyes - there to remain, forgotten by the gay circles in which I moved for a brief season."

"Dear heart! will you not be quiet?" said Mrs. Loring; laying her fingers once more upon her lips.

Mrs. Dexter sighed as her lashes drooped upon her cheeks. Very still she lay after this, and as her aunt stood looking upon her white, shrunken face and hollow eyes, and noted the purple stain on her cheek and temple, tears of compassion filled her eyes, and tender pity softened all her feelings.

That night Jessie slept in her aunt's room. Morning found her in a calmer state, and with less prostration of body than Mrs. Loring had feared would ensue. She did not rise until late, but met her cousins while yet in bed, with a quiet warmth of manner that placed both them and herself at ease with one another, They bad been frightened witnesses of the exciting scenes in the parlor, when Mrs. Dexter twice confronted her husband and met his intimations of wrong with indignant denial. Beyond this their mother had informed them that their cousin had left her home and might not again return to it. For the present she enjoined silence as to what had occurred; and reserve or evasion of questions should curious inquirers approach them at school or elsewhere.

Before Jessie had arisen, Mr. Dexter called. He looked worn and troubled. It was plain that his night had been sleepless.

"How is she?" he asked of Mrs. Loring, almost fearfully, as if dreading the answer. He did not pronounce the name of his wife.

"Better than I had hoped," was replied.

"Has she required the attention of a physician?"

"No."

Mr. Dexter seemed relieved.

"What is her state of mind?"

"She is more tranquil than I had expected to find her."

Mrs. Loring's manner was cold.

"Have you conversed with her this morning?"

"But little."

"Will she see me?"

"I think not."

"Will you ask her?"

"Not now. She is too weak to bear a recurrence of agitating scenes."

Mr. Dexter bit his lips firmly as if striving with his feelings.

"When can I see her?"

"That question I am unable now to answer, Mr. Dexter. But my own opinion is that it will be better for you to see her to-morrow than to-day: better next week than to-morrow. You must give time for calmness and reflection."

"She is my wife!" exclaimed Mr. Dexter, not able to control himself. The manner in which this was said conveyed clearly his thought to Mrs. Loring, and she replied with equal feeling -

"But not your slave to command!"

"Madam! I warn you not to enter into this league against me - not to become a party in this wicked scheme! If you do, then you must bear the consequences of such blind folly. I am not the man to submit tamely. I will not submit."

"You are simply beating the air," replied Mrs. Loring. "There is no league against you - no wicked scheme - nothing beyond your own excited imagination; and I warn you, in turn, not to proceed one step further in this direction."

"Madam! can I see my wife?" The attitude of Mr. Dexter was threatening.

"No, sir. Not now," was the firmly spoken answer.

He turned to go.

"Mr. Dexter."

"Well? Say on."

"I do not wish you to call here again."

"Madam! my wife is harboring here."

"I will give my servant orders not to admit you!" said Mrs.

Loring, outraged by this remark.

For an instant Dexter looked as if he would destroy her, were it in his power, by a single glance; then turning away he left the house, muttering impotent threats.

And so the breach grew wider.

"I don't wonder that Jessie could not live with him," said Mrs. Loring to herself. "Such a temper! Dear heart! Who can tell how much she may have suffered?"

CHAPTER XXI

ONCE more Jessie found herself alone in the little chamber where her gentle girlish life, had strengthened towards womanhood. Many times had she visited this chamber since her marriage, going to it as to some pilgrim-shrine, but never with the feelings that now crowded upon her heart. She had returned as a dove, to the ark from the wild waste of waters, wing-weary, faint, frightened - fluttering into this holy place, conscious of safety. She was not to go out again. Blessed thought! How it warmed the life-blood in her heart, and sent the currents in more genial streams through every vein.

But alas! memory could not die. Lethe was only a fable of the olden times. A place of safety is not always a place of freedom from pain. It could not be so in this instance. Yet, for a time, like the exhausted prisoner borne back from torture to his cell, the crushed members reposed in delicious insensibility. The hard pallet was a heaven of ease to the iron rack on which the quivering flesh had been torn, and the joints wrenched, until nature cried out in agony.

Dear little room! Though its walls were narrow, and its furniture simple even to meagreness, it was a palace in her regard to the luxurious chambers she had left. It was all her own. She need not veil her heart there. No semblances were required. No intrusion feared. It seemed to her, for a time, as if she had been so lifted out of the world, as to be no longer a part of it. The hum and shock of men were far below her. She had neither part nor lot in common humanity.

But this could not last. She had formed relations with that world not to be cast off lightly. She was a wife, violently separated from her husband; and setting at defiance the laws which had bound them together.

On the third day Mrs. Dexter received a communication from her husband. It was imperative, reading thus:

"MRS. DEXTER - I have twice sought to gain an interview, and twice been repelled with insult. I now write to ask when and where you will see me. We must meet, Jessie. This rash step, I fear, is going to involve consequences far more disastrous than you have imagined. It is no light thing for a woman to throw herself beyond the pale of her husband's protection. - Something is owed to the world - something to reputation - something to your good name; and much to your husband. I may have been hasty, but I was sincere. There are some things that looked wrong; *they look wrong still*, and will *always look wrong* if your present attitude is maintained. I wish to see you, that we may, together, review these unhappy questions, and out of a tangled skein bring even threads, if possible. Let me hear from you immediately.

"YOUR HUSBAND."

Twice Mrs. Dexter read this letter, hurriedly at first, but very slowly the second time; weighing each word and sentence carefully. She then laid it aside, and almost crouching down in her chair, fell into such deep thought that she seemed more like one sleeping than awake. She did not attempt an answer until the next day. Then she penned the following:

"To LEON DEXTER - In leaving your house and your protection, I was not governed by caprice or impulse. For some time I have seen that, sooner or later, it must come to this; that the cord uniting us was too severely strained, and must snap. I did not suppose the time so near at hand - that you would drag upon it now with such a sudden force. But the deed is done, and we are apart forever. I cannot live with you again - your presence would suffocate me. There was a mutual wrong in our marriage; but I was most to blame; for I knew that I did not and never could love you as I believed a husband should be loved. But you had extorted from me a promise of marriage, and I believed it to be my duty to fulfill that promise. Young, inexperienced, blind to the future, I took up the burdens you laid at my feet, and believed myself strong enough to carry them all the days of my life. It was a fatal error. How painfully I have struggled on - how prayerfully, how patiently, how self-denyingly, you can never know. Yet, without avail. I have fallen by the way, and there is not strength enough in me to lift the burdens again. I know this, and One besides; and I am content to rest the case with Him. The world will blame - the church censure - the law condemn. Let it be so. All that is light to the sufferings I have endured, and from which I have fled.

"I cannot see you, Mr. Dexter - *I will not see you.* Our ways in this world have parted, and forever. The act was not mine, but yours. You flung me off with a force that overcame all scruple - all question of right - all effort to cling to you as my husband. I was trying, in my feeble way - for not much power remained - to be a dutiful wife, when you extinguished all hope of success by a charge as false as the evil spirit who whispered in your too willing ears a suspicion of infidelity against one who had never permitted a thought of wrong towards her husband to enter even the outermost portal of her mind. I had not seen the person to whom you allude since my accidental meeting with him at Newport, so basely construed into design; and his passing my window at the moment you returned home, was as unexpected to me as to you.

"I had hoped that my previous solemn assurances were sufficient to give you confidence in my integrity. But this was an error. You had no faith in me; and assailed me with violence when my thoughts were as true to honor as ever were yours. Did you imagine that I could lie passive at your feet, so trampled down and degraded? No, sir! God gave me a higher consciousness - a purer spirit - a nobler individuality! You should have mated one of a different stamp from me!

"And yet I pity you, Leon Dexter! This web of trouble, which your own hands have woven around your life, will fetter and gall you at every step in your future journey. I have not left you in a spirit of retaliation; but simply because the natural strain of repulsion was stronger than all the attractive forces that held us together. I only obeyed a law against which weak nature strove in vain. Were it in my power, I would make all your future bright with the warmest sunshine. But over your future I have no control - yet, sadly enough, are our destinies linked, and the existence of each will be a thorn in the other's heart.

"I have not much strength left. The contest has nearly extinguished my life. This is the last struggle I shall have with you. My first weak thought was to return your letter without a word in reply. But that would have been a wrong to both; and so I have made you this communication, and you must regard it as final. Farewell, unhappy Leon Dexter! I would have saved you from this calamity, but you would not let me! May He who has permitted you thus to drag down the temple of domestic happiness, and bury yourself amid the ruins, give you, in this direful calamity, a higher than human power of endurance. May the fierce flames of this great ordeal, find gold in your character beyond the reach of fire. Farewell, forever! and may God bless and keep you! The prayer is from a heart yet free from guile, and the lips that breathe it upward are as pure as when you laid upon them the marriage kiss! God keep them as guileless and as pure! Amen!

"JESSIE."

Dexter accepted the decision of his wife as final. What else was

T.S. Arthur

left for him? He would have been the dullest of men not to have seen the spirit of this answer, shining everywhere through the letter. Something more than feebly dawned the conviction in his mind, that he had foully wronged his wife, and that the fearful calamity which had overtaken him in the morning of his days, was of his own creating. He did not again attempt to see her; made no further remonstrance; offered no kind of annoyance. A profound respect for the suffering woman who had abandoned him, took the place of indignation against her. In silence he sat down amid his crushed hopes and broken idols, and waited for light to guide him and strength to walk onward. Like thousands of other men, he had discovered that a human soul was not a plaything, nor a piece of machinery to wind up and set in motion at will; and like thousands of other men, he had made this discovery too late.

CHAPTER XXII

WITHOUT a note of warning, the public were startled by the news that Mrs. Dexter had left her husband. Wisely, sober second thought laid upon the lips of Mr. Dexter the seal of silence. He gave no reason for the step his wife had taken, and declined answering all inquiries, even from his nearest friends. From a man of impulse, he seemed changed at once into a man of deliberate purpose. His elegant home was not given up, though he lived in it a kind of half hermit life. Abroad, he was reserved; while everything about him gave signs of a painful inward conflict.

Of course, the social air was full of rumors, probable and improbable, but none of them exactly true. Mrs. Dexter was wholly silent, except to her wisest and truest friend, Mrs. De Lisle - and her discretion ever kept her guarded. Mrs. Loring simply alleged "incompatibility of temper" - that vague allegation which covers with its broad mantle so wide a range of domestic antagonisms. And so the public had its appetite piqued, and the nine days' wonder became the wonder of a season. Hints towards the truth were embellished by gossips' ready imaginations, and stories of wrong, domestic (sic) tyranny, infidelity, and the like, were passed around, and related with a degree of circumstantiality that gave them wide credence. Yet in no instance was the name of Hendrickson connected with that of Mrs. Dexter. So transient had been their intercourse, that no eye but that of jealousy had noted their meeting as anything beyond the meeting of indifferent acquaintances.

It was just one week from the day Paul Hendrickson caught an unexpected glimpse of Mrs. Dexter's face at the window, and passed on with her image freshened in his heart, that he called in at the Ardens', after an unusually long absence, to spend an evening. Miss Arden's countenance lighted with a sudden glow on his appearance, the rich blood dyeing her cheeks, and giving her face a heightened charm; and in the visitor's eyes there was something gentler and softer in her beauty than he had before observed. He probably guessed the cause; and the thought touched his feelings, and drew his heart something nearer to her.

"That is a painful story about Mrs. Dexter," said Mrs. Arden, almost as soon as the young man came in. The recently heard facts were uppermost in her thoughts.

"What story? I have not heard anything." Hendrickson was on his guard in a moment; though he betrayed unusual interest.

"It is dreadful to think of!" said Miss Arden. "What a wretched creature she must be! I always thought her one of the best of women. Though I must own that at Saratoga last summer, she showed rather more fondness for the society of other men than she did for that of her husband."

"I am still in the dark," said Mr. Hendrickson, with suppressed excitement.

"Then you haven't heard of it? Why, it's the town talk."

"No."

"There's been a separation between Mrs. Dexter and her husband," remarked Mrs. Arden. "She left him several days ago, and is now with her aunt, Mrs. Loring."

"A separation! On what ground?" Hendrickson's breathing oppressed him.

"Something wrong with Mrs. Dexter, I am told. She had too many admirers - so the story goes; and, worse still - for admiration she couldn't help - one lover."

It was Mrs. Arden who said this.

"Who was the lover?" asked Mr. Hendrickson. His voice was so quiet, and his tones so indifferent, that none suspected the intense interest with which he was listening.

"I have not heard his name," replied Mrs. Arden.

"Does he live in this city?"

"I believe not. Some new acquaintance, made at Newport, I think. You remember that she was very ill there last summer?"

"Yes."

"Well, the cause of that illness is now said to have been a discovery by Mr. Dexter of some indiscretion on her part, followed by angry remonstrance on his."

"That is the story?"

"Yes."

"And what caused the separation which has just taken place?"

"A renewal of this intimacy," said Mrs. Arden.

"A very serious charge; and, I believe without foundation in truth," replied Hendrickson. He spoke slowly, yet not with strong emphasis. His auditors did not know that he was simply controlling his voice to hide his agitation.

"Oh, there is no doubt as to its truth," said Mrs. Arden. "The facts have been substantiated; so Mrs. Anthony told me to-day; and she has been one of Mrs. Dexter's most intimate friends."

"What facts?" inquired Hendrickson.

"Facts, that if they do not prove crime against Mrs. Dexter, show her to have been imprudent to the verge of crime."

"Can you particularize?" said the young man.

"Well, no I can't just do that. Mrs. Anthony ran on at such a rate that I couldn't get the affair adjusted in my mind. But she asserts positively that Mrs. Dexter has gone considerably beyond the boundary of prudence; and she is no friend of Dexter's, I can assure you. As far as I can learn, there have been frequent meetings between this lover and Mrs. Dexter during the husband's absence. An earlier return home, a few days ago, led to a surprise and an exposure. The result you know."

"I must make bold to pronounce this whole story a fabrication," said Mr. Hendrickson, with rising warmth; "It is too improbable."

"Worse things than that have happened, and are happening every day," remarked Mrs. Arden.

"Still I shall disbelieve the story," said Mr. Hendrickson, firmly.

"What else would justify him in sending her home to her aunt?" asked Mrs. Arden.

"He sent her home, then? That is the report?" remarked Hendrickson.

"Some say one thing and some another."

"And a story loses nothing in the repetition."

"You are very skeptical," said Miss Arden.

"I wish all men and women were more skeptical than they are, in touching the wrong doings of others," replied the young man. "The world is not so bad as it seems. Now I am sure that if the truth of this affair could really be known, we should find scarcely a single fact in agreement with the report. I have heard that Mr. Dexter is blindly jealous of his wife."

"Oh, as to that, Mrs. Anthony says that he made himself ridiculous by his jealousy at Saratoga last summer. And I now remember that he used to act strangely sometimes," said Mrs. Arden.

"A jealous man," returned Hendrickson, "is a very bad judge of his wife's conduct; and more likely to see guilt than innocence in any circumstance that will bear a double explanation. Let us then lean to the side of charity, and suppose good until the proof of evil stares us in the very face; as I shall do in this instance. I have always believed Mrs. Dexter to be the purest of women; and I believe so still."

Both Mrs. Arden and her daughter seemed annoyed at this defence of a woman against whom they had so readily accepted the common rumor. But they said nothing farther. After that an unusual embarrassment marked their intercourse. As early as he could, with politeness, retire, Hendrickson went away. He did not err in his own elucidation of the mystery; for he remembered well the vision of Mrs. Dexter's face at the window - her instant sign of feeling - his own quick but not meditated response - and the sudden appearance of her husband, whose clouded countenance was full of angry suspicion.

"To this! - and so soon!" said Hendrickson to himself, as he left the house of Mrs. Arden. "Oh, that I could stretch out my hand to save her! - That I could shield her from the tempests! - That I could shelter her from the burning heats! But I cannot. There is a great gulf between us, and I may not pass to her, nor she to me. Oh, my soul! is this separation to be for all time?"

There was rebellion in the heart of Paul Hendrickson when he reached his home; and a wild desire to overleap all barriers of separation.

"There will be a divorce in all probability," so he began talking with himself. "Jessie will never return to him after this violent separation; and he, after a time, will ask to have the marriage annulled. He will not be able to bring proof of evil against her - will, I am sure, not even attempt it; for no evidence exists. But her steady refusal to live with him as his wife, will enable him, it may be, to get a divorce. And then!"

There was a tone of exultation in his voice at the closing words.

"And whosoever marrieth her which is put away, committeth adultery."

Hendrickson started to his feet, his face as pale as ashes, and glanced almost fearfully about the room. The voice seemed spoken in the air - but it was not so. The warning had reached his sense of hearing by an inner way.

Then he sat down, and pondered this new question, so suddenly presented for solution, turning it towards every light - viewing it now from the side of human feeling and human reason - and now with the light of Divine Revelation shining upon it. But he was not satisfied. The letter of the record was against him; but nature cried out for some different reading. At length he made an effort to thrust the subject aside.

"What folly is this?" he said, still talking with himself. "Wait! wait! wait! - the time is not yet. Separation only exists. There is no divorce. The great, impassable gulf is yet between us. I cannot go to her. She cannot come to me. I must wait, hopefully, if not patiently, the issue of events."

The thoughts of Hendrickson had once more been turning themselves towards Miss Arden, and he had felt the glow of warmer feelings. He had even begun to think again of marriage.

"Let that illusion go!" he said. "It must no longer tempt me to the commission of an act that reason and conscience both pronounce wrong. I do not love Mary Arden; therefore, I will not marry her. I settle that matter now, and forever."

And the decision was final. He did not visit her again for many months, and then only after her engagement to another.

CHAPTER XXIII

THERE were plenty of intrusive friends to give Mr. Dexter advice as to how he should act towards the unhappy woman who had fled from him in her despair. He was rich, good-hearted - as the world goes - honorable, domestic in his feelings and habits; everything, in fact, that society requires in the composition of a good husband. The blame, therefore, among the friends of Mr. Dexter, was all on the side of his wife.

"You will, of course, if she persists in this unwarrantable conduct, demand a legal separation," said one.

"That is just what she wants," suggested another. "You could not grant her a higher favor."

"Wait - wait," was the advice of a third.

And so the changes were rung. Dexter listened, pondered, suffered; but admitted no one into the council chamber of his heart. There were some things known only to himself and the one he had driven from him, which he did not care to reveal. The shock of separation had rent away a few scales from his eyes, and his vision was clearer; but the clearer vision did not lessen his misery - for self-upbraidings crowded in with the illustrating light.

For a while, jealous suspicion kept him watchfully alive to the movements of Paul Hendrickson. In order to gain the most undoubted information in regard to him, he secured the services of an intelligent policeman, who, well paid for his work, kept so sharp an eye upon him, that he was able to report his whereabouts for almost every hour of the day and evening.

Days, weeks, months even passed, and the policeman's report varied scarcely a sentence. The range of Hendrickson's movements was from his place of business to his lodgings. Once a week, perhaps, he went out in the evening; but never were his steps directed to the neighborhood in which the object of his waking and dreaming thoughts resided.

In part, this knowledge of Hendrickson's mode of living relieved the mind of Dexter; yet, when viewed in certain lights, it proved a cause of deeper disturbance. His conclusions in the case were near the truth. Hendrickson's withdrawal of himself from society - his hermit-like life - his sober face and musing aspect - seemed only so many evidences of his undying love for Mrs. Dexter. That an impassable barrier existed (sic) betwen them - that, as things were, even a friendly intercourse would be next to crime - Hendrickson felt; and Dexter's clearer perceptions awarded him a just conclusion in this particular.

So far as Mrs. Dexter was concerned, the heavy curtain that fell so suddenly between her and the world was not drawn aside - not uplifted - even for a moment. Her deep seclusion of herself was nun-like. Gradually new objects of interest - new causes of excitement - pressed the thought of her aside, and her name grew a less and less familiar sound in fashionable and family circles. Some thought of her as a wronged woman - some as a guilty woman - yet all with a degree of sympathy.

A year Mr. Dexter waited for some sign from his wife. But if the grave had closed over her, the isolation from him could not have been more perfect. He then sold his house, removed to a hotel, and made preparations for an absence in Europe of indefinite continuance. He went, and was gone for over two years. - Returned, and almost immediately on his arrival, took legal steps for procuring a divorce. Mrs. Dexter received due notice of these proceedings, based simply on her abandonment of her husband, and refusal to live with him as a wife. But she remained entirely passive. The proceedings went on, and in due time Mr. Dexter obtained what he sought, a divorce. Within a month after the decree in his favor, he returned across the Atlantic.

The publication of this decree awakened a brief interest in Mrs. Dexter - or rather in plain Jessie Loring, as she was now in legal aspect. But the curious public were not able to acquire any satisfactory information in regard to her. The world in which she lived was a *terra incognita* to them.

The next exciting news which came in this connection, was the announcement of Dexter's marriage with an English heiress. He did not return with her to the United States; but remained in England, where he established a foreign branch of the mercantile house in which he was a partner, and took up his permanent residence beyond the sea.

CHAPTER XXIV

Six years from the day Jessie Loring laid her bleeding heart on the marriage altar had passed. For over three years of that time she had not stepped beyond the threshold of her aunt's dwelling, and only at rare intervals was she seen by visitors. She had not led an idle life, however; else would her days long ere this have been numbered. To her aunt and cousins she had, from the day of her return, devoted herself, in all things wherein she could aid, counsel, minister, or sustain; and that with so much of patient cheerfulness, and loving self-devotion, that she had become endeared to them beyond any former attachment. There was an odor of goodness about her life that made her presence an incentive to right action.

Long before this period, Mrs. Loring had ceased all efforts to lead Jessie out of her self-imposed seclusion.

"Not yet, dear aunt! Not yet," was the invariable answer.

The day on which she received formal notice that her husband had applied for a divorce, she shut herself up in her room, and did not leave it, nor hold communion with any one, until the next morning. Then, with the exception of a wearied look, as if she had not slept well, and a shade of sadness about her lips, no change was discernible. When the decree, annulling the marriage between her and Dexter, was placed in her hands, she seemed bewildered for a time, as if she found it almost impossible to realize her new position.

T.S. Arthur

"I congratulate you, Jessie Loring!" said her aunt, speaking from her external view of the case. "You are free again. Free as the wind!"

"This does not place me where I was," Jessie replied.

"Why not? The law has cancelled your marriage!" said Mrs. Loring. "You stand in your old relation to the world."

"But not to myself," Jessie answered with a deep sigh; and leaving her aunt, she went away to her little chamber, there to sit in solemn debate over this new aspect of affairs in her troubled life.

No - no. She did not stand in her old relation to herself. She was not a maiden with lips free from the guile of a false marriage promise; but a divorced wife. A thing questionably recognized, both in human opinion and divine law. Deeply and solemnly did this conviction weigh upon her thoughts. View the case in any of the lights which shone into her mind, she could not discover an aspect that gave her real comfort. It is true she was free from all legal obligations to her former husband, and that was something gained. But what of that husband's position under the literal reading of the divine law? No doubt he contemplated marriage. But could he marry, conscience clear? Had not her false vows cursed both their lives? - imposed on each almost impossible necessities?

Such were the questions that thrust themselves upon her, and clamored for solution.

She had not solved them when the intelligence came of Mr. Dexter's marriage in England.

"I have news that will surprise you," said Mrs. Loring, coming into the sitting-room where Jessie was at work on a piece of embroidery.

"What is it?" she asked, looking up almost with a start, for something in her aunt's manner told her that she had a personal interest in the news.

"Mr. Dexter is married!"

Instantly a pallor overspread Jessie's face.

"Married to an English lady," said Mrs. Loring.

Jessie looked at her aunt for a little while, but without a remark. She then turned her eyes again upon her embroidery, lifting it close to her face. But her hand trembled so that she could not take a stitch.

"I hope he's satisfied now," said Mrs. Loring. "He's married an heiress - so the story goes; and is going to reside with her in England. I'm glad of that any how. It might not be so pleasant for you to meet them - sensitive thing that you are! But it wouldn't trouble *me*. *I* could look them both in the face and not blink. Much joy may he have with his English bride! Bless me, child, how you do tremble!" she added, as she noticed the fingers of her niece trying in vain to direct the needle she held upon the face of the embroidery. "It's nothing more than you had to expect. And, besides, what is Leon Dexter to you now? Only as another man?"

Jessie arose without speaking, and kissing her aunt in token of love, passed quickly from the room.

"Dear! dear! what a strange child it is!" said Aunt Loring, as she wiped off a tear which had fallen from Jessie's eyes upon her cheek. "Just like her mother for all the world in some things" - the last part of the sentence was in a qualifying tone - "though," she went on, "her mother hadn't anything like her trials to endure. Oh, that Dexter! if I only had my will of him!"

And Aunt Loring, in her rising indignation, actually clenched her hand and shook it in the air.

"It has come to this at last," said Jessie as soon as she had gained the sanctuary of her little chamber, where she could think without interruption. "And I knew it must come; but oh, how I have dreaded the event! Is he innocent in the sight of heaven? Ah, if I could only have that question answered in the affirmative, a crushing weight would be lifted from my soul. If he is not innocent, the stain of his guilt rests upon my garments! He is not alone responsible. Who can tell the consequences of a single false step in life?"

From a small hanging shelf she took a Bible, and opening to a marked page, read over three or four verses with earnest attention.

"I can see no other meaning," she said with a painful sigh, closing the book and restoring it to its place on the shelf. It was all in vain that Jessie Loring sought for light and comfort in this direction. They were not found. When she joined her aunt, some hours afterwards, her face had not regained its former placidity.

"Well, dear," said Mrs. Loring, speaking in what sounded to the ear of her niece a light tone, "have you got it all right with yourself?"

Jessie smiled faintly, and merely answered -

"It will take time. But I trust that all will come out truly adjusted in the end."

She had never ventured to bring to her aunt's very external judgment the real questions that troubled her. Mrs. Loring's prompt way of sweeping aside these cobwebs of the brain, as she called the finer scruples of conscience, could not satisfy her yearning desire for light.

"Yes; time works wonders. He is the great restorer. But why not see clearly at once; and not wait in suffering for time's slow movements? I am a wiser philosopher than you are, Jessie; and try to gain from the present all that it has to give."

"Some hearts require a severer discipline than others," said Jessie. "And mine, I think, is one of them."

"All that is sickly sentiment, my dear child! as I have said to you a hundred times. It is not shadow, but sunshine that your heart wants - not discipline, but consolation - not doubt, but hope. You are as untrue to yourself as the old anchorites. These self-inflicted stripes are horrible to think of, for the pain is not salutary, but only increases the morbid states of mind that ever demand new flagellations."

"We are differently made, Aunt Phoebe," was the quiet answer.

"No, we are not, but we make ourselves different," replied Mrs. Loring a little hastily.

"The world would be a very dead-level affair, if we were all made alike," said Jessie, forcing a smile, and assuming a lighter air, in order to lead her aunt's mind away from the thought of her as too painfully disturbed by the announcement of Mr. Dexter's marriage. And she was successful. The subject was changed to one of a less embarrassing character. And this was all of the inner life of Jessie Loring that showed itself on the surface.

CHAPTER XXV

AND what of Paul Hendrickson during these years of isolation, in which no intelligence could be gained of Jessie, beyond vague rumors? For a time, he secluded himself. Then he returned to a few of the old social circles, not much changed to the common eye. His countenance was a little graver; his voice a little lower; his manner a trifle more subdued. But he was a cheerful, intelligent companion, and always a welcome guest.

To no one, not even to his old friend, Mrs. Denison, did he speak of Mrs. Dexter. What right had he to speak of her? She was still the lawful wife of another man, though separated from him by her own act. But not to think of her was as impossible as not to think at all - not to gaze upon her image as impossible as to extinguish the inner vision. She was always by his side, in spirit; her voice always in his ears; her dear face always before him. "The cup is dashed to pieces at my feet, and the precious wine spilled!" How many, many, many times, each day, did he hear these words uttered, always in that sad, half-desponding voice that first brought the m to his ears; and they kept hope in the future alive.

The separation which had taken place Hendrickson regarded as one step in the right direction. When the application for a divorce was made, he hailed it with a degree of inward satisfaction that a little startled himself. "It is another step in the right direction," he said, on the instant's impulse.

Reflection a little sobered him. "Even if the divorce is granted, what will be her views of the matter?"

There came no satisfactory answer to this query.

A thick curtain still veiled the future. Many doubts troubled him.

Next, in the order of events, came the decision by which the marriage contract between Dexter and his wife was annulled. On the evening of the same day on which the court granted the petitioner's prayer, Hendrickson called upon Mrs. Denison. She saw the moment he came in that he was excited about something.

"Have you heard the news?" he inquired.

"What news?" Mrs. Denison looked at him curiously.

"Leon Dexter has obtained a divorce."

"Has he?"

"Yes. And so that long agony is over! She is free again."

Hendrickson was not able to control the intense excitement he felt.

Mrs. Denison looked at him soberly and with glances of inquiry.

"You understand me, I suppose?"

"Perhaps I do, perhaps not," she answered.

"Mrs. Denison," said the young man, with increasing excitement, "I need scarcely say to you that my heart has never swerved from its first idolatry. To love Jessie Loring was an instinct of my nature - therefore, to love her once was to love her forever. You know how cruelly circumstances came with their impassable barriers. They were only barriers, and destroyed nothing. As brightly as ever burned the fires - as ardently as ever went forth love's strong impulses with every heart-beat. And her heart remained true to mine as ever was needle to the pole."

"That is a bold assertion, Paul," said Mrs. Denison, "and one that it pains me to hear you make."

"It is true; but why does it give you pain?" he asked.

"Because it intimates the existence of an understanding between you and Mrs. Dexter, and looks to the confirmation of rumors that I have always considered as without a shadow of foundation."

"My name has never been mentioned in connection with hers."

"It has."

"Mrs. Denison!"

"It is true."

"I never heard it."

"Nor I but once."

"What was said?"

"That you were the individual against whom Mr. Dexter's jealousy was excited, and that your clandestine meetings with his wife led to the separation."

"I had believed," said Hendrickson, after a pause, and in a voice that showed a depression of feeling, "that busy rumor had never joined our names together. That it has done so, I deeply regret. No voluntary action of mine led to this result; and it was my opinion that Dexter had carefully avoided any mention of my name, even to his most intimate friends."

"I only heard the story once, and then gave it my emphatic denial," said Mrs. Denison.

"And yet it was true, I believe, though in a qualified sense. We did meet, not clandestinely, however, nor with design."

"But without a thought, much less a purpose of dishonor," said Mrs. Denison, almost severely.

"Without even a thought of dishonor," replied Hendrickson. "Both were incapable of that. She arrived at Newport when I was there. We met, suddenly and unexpectedly, face to face, and when off our guard. I read her heart, and she read mine, in lightning glimpses. The pages were shut instantly, and not opened again. We met once or twice after that, but as mere acquaintances, and I left on the day after she came, because I saw that the discipline was too severe for her, and that I was not only in an equivocal, but dangerous, if not dishonorable position. Dexter had his eyes on me all the while, and if I crossed his path suddenly he looked as if he would have destroyed me with a glance. The fearful illness, which came so near extinguishing the life of Mrs. Dexter, was, I have never doubted, in consequence of that meeting and circumstances springing directly therefrom. A friend of mine had a room adjoining theirs at Newport, and he once said to me, without imagining my interest in the case, that on the day before Mrs. Dexter's illness was known, he had heard her voice pitched to a higher key than usual, and had caught a few words that too clearly indicated a feeling of outrage for some perpetrated wrong. There was stern defiance also, he said, in her tones. He was pained at the circumstance, for he had met Mrs. Dexter frequently, he said, at Newport, and was charmed with her fine intelligence and womanly attractions.

"Once after that we looked into each other's faces, and only once. And then, as before, we read the secret known only to ourselves - but without design. I was passing her residence - it was the first time I had permitted myself even to go into the neighborhood where she lived, since her return from Newport. Now something drew me that way, and yielding to the impulse, I took the street on which her dwelling stood, and ere a thought of honor checked my footsteps, was by her door. A single glance at one of the parlor windows gave me the vision of her pale face, so attenuated by sickness and suffering, that the sight filled me with instant pity, and fired my soul with a deeper love. What my countenance expressed I do not know. It must have betrayed my feelings, for I was off my guard. Her face was as the page of a book suddenly opened. I read it without losing the meaning of a word. There was a painful sequel to this. The husband of Mrs. Dexter, as if he had started from the ground, confronted me on the instant. Which way he came - whether he had followed me, or advanced by an opposite direction, I know not. But there he stood, and his flashing eyes read both of our unveiled faces. The expression of his countenance was almost fiendish.

"I passed on, without pause or start. Nothing more than the answering glances he had seen was betrayed. But the consequences were final. It was on that day that Mrs. Dexter left her husband, never again to hold with him any communication. I have scarcely dared permit myself to imagine what transpired on that occasion. The outrage on his part must have been extreme, or the desperate alternative of abandonment would never have been taken by such a woman.

"There, my good friend and aforetime counsellor," added Hendrickson, "you have the unvarnished story. A stern necessity drew around each of us bands of iron. Yet we have been true to ourselves - and that means true to honor. But now the darker features of the case are changed. She is no longer the wife of Leon Dexter. The law has shattered every link of the accursed chain that held her in such a loathsome bondage."

He paused, for the expression of Mrs. Denison's countenance

was not by any means satisfactory.

"Right, so far," said Mrs. Denison. "I cannot see that either was guilty of wrong, or even, imprudence. But I am afraid, Paul, that you are springing to conclusions with too bold a leap."

"Do not say that, Mrs. Denison."

He spoke quickly, and with a suddenly shadowed face.

"Your meaning is very plain," was answered. "It is this. A divorce having been granted to the prayer of Mr. Dexter, his wife is now free to marry again."

"Yes, that is my meaning," said Hendrickson, looking steadily into the face of Mrs. Denison. She merely shook her head in a grave, quiet way.

Hendrickson drew a long breath, then compressed his lips - but still looked into the face of his friend.

"There are impediments yet in the way," said Mrs. Denison.

"I know what you think. The Divine law is superior to all human enactments."

"Is it not so, Paul?"

"If I was certain as to the Divine law," said Hendrickson.

"The record is very explicit."

"Read in the simple letter, I grant that it is. But" -

"Paul! It grieves me to throw an icy chill over your ardent feelings," said Mrs. Denison, interrupting him. "But you may rest well assured of one thing: Jessie Loring, though no longer Mrs. Dexter, will not consider herself free to marry again."

"Do you know her views on this subject?" asked the young man, quickly.

"I think I know the woman. In the spirit of a martyr she took up her heavy cross, and bore it while she had strength to stand. The martyr spirit is not dead in her. It will not die while life remains. In the fierce ordeals through which she has passed, she has learned to endure; and now weak nature must yield, if in any case opposed to duty."

"Have you met her of late?" inquired the young man, curiously.

"No, but I talked with Mrs. De Lisle about her not long ago. Mrs. De Lisle is her most intimate friend, and knows her better, perhaps, than any other living person."

"And what does she say? Have you conversed with her on this subject?"

"No; but I have learned enough from her in regard to Jessie's views of life and duty, as well as states of religious feeling, to be justified in saying that she will not consider a court's decree of sufficient authority in the case. Alas! my young friend, I cannot see cause for gratulation so far as you are concerned. To her, the act of divorce (sic) way give a feeling of relief. A dead weight is stricken from her limbs. She can walk and breathe more freely; but she will not consider herself wholy untrammelled. Nor would I. Paul, Paul! the gulf that separates you is still impassable! But do not despair! Bear up bravely, manfully still. Six years of conflict, discipline, and stern obedience to duty have made you more worthy of a union with that pure spirit than you were when you saw her borne from your eager, outstretched arms. Her mind is ripening heaven-ward - let yours ripen in that direction also. You cannot mate with her, my friend, in the glorious hereafter, unless you are of equal purity. Oh, be patient, yet hopeful!"

Hendrickson had bowed his head, and was now sitting with

his eyes upon the floor. He did not answer after Mrs. Denison ceased speaking, but still sat deeply musing.

"It is a hard saying!" He had raised his eyes to the face of his maternal friend. "A hard saying, and hard to bear. Oh, there is something so like the refinement of cruelty in these stern events which hold us apart, that I feel at times like questioning the laws that imposed such fearful restrictions. We are one in all the essentials of marriage, Mrs. Denison. Why are we thus sternly held apart?"

"It is one of the necessities of our fallen nature," Mrs. Denison replied, in her calm, yet earnest voice, "that spiritual virtues can only have birth in pain. We rise into the higher regions of heavenly purity only after the fires have tried us. Some natures, as you know, demand a severer discipline than others. Yours, I think, is one of them. Jessie's is another. But after the earthly dross of your souls is consumed, the pure gold will flow together, I trust, at the bottom of the same crucible. Wait, my friend; wait longer. The time is not yet."

A sadder man than when he came, did Mr. Hendrickson leave the house of Mrs. Denison on that day. She had failed to counsel him according to his wishes; but her words, though they had not carried full conviction to his clouded under- standing, had shown him a goal still far in advance, towards which all of true manhood in him felt the impulse to struggle.

CHAPTER XXVI

WHEN the news of Mr. Dexter's second marriage reached Mr. Hendrickson, he said:

"Now she is absolved!" but his friend Mrs. Denison, replied:

"I doubt if she will so consider it. No act of Mr. Dexter's can alter her relation to the Divine law. I am one of these who cannot regard him as wholly innocent. And yet his case is an extreme one; for his wife's separation was as final as if death had broken the bond. But I will not judge him; he is the keeper of his own conscience, and the All-Wise is merciful in construction."

"I believe Jessie Loring to be as free to give her hand as before her marriage."

"With her will rest the decision," was Mrs. Denison's answer.

"Have you seen her?" inquired Hendrickson.

"No."

"Has she been seen outside of her aunt's dwelling?"

"If so I have never heard of it."

"Do you think, if I were to call at Mrs. Loring's, she would see me?"

"I cannot answer the question."

"But what is your opinion?"

"If I were you," said Mrs. Denison, "I would not call at present."

"Why."

"This act of her former husband is too recent. Let her have time to get her mind clear as to her new relation. She may break through her seclusion now, and go abroad into society again. If so you will meet her without the constraint of a private interview."

"But she may still shut herself out from the world. Isolation may have become a kind of second nature."

"We shall see," replied Mrs. Denison. "But for the present I think it will be wiser to wait."

Weeks, even months, passed, and Paul Hendrickson waited in vain. He was growing very impatient.

"I must see her! Suspense like this is intolerable!" he said, coming in upon Mrs. Denison one evening.

"I warn you against it," replied Mrs. Denison.

"I cannot heed the warning."

"Her life is very placid, I am told by Mrs. De Lisle. Would you throw its elements again into wild disturbance?"

"No; I would only give them their true activity. All is stagnation now. I would make her life one thrill of conscious joy."

"I have conversed with Mrs. De Lisle on this subject," said Mrs. Denison.

"You have? And what does she say?"

"She understands the whole case. I concealed nothing - was I right?"

"Yes. But go on."

"She does not think that Jessie will marry during the lifetime of Mr. Dexter," said Mrs. Denison.

Hendrickson became pale.

"I fear," he remarked, "that I did not read her heart aright. I thought that we were conjoined in spirit. Oh, if I have been in error here, the wreck is hopeless!"

He showed a sudden and extreme depression.

"I think you have not erred, Paul. But if Jessie regards the conditions of divorce, given in Matthew, as binding, she is too pure and true a woman ever to violate them. All depends upon that. She could not be happy with you, if her conscience were burdened with the conviction that your marriage was not legal in the Divine sense. Don't you see how such an act would depress her? Don't you see that, in gaining her, you would sacrifice the brightest jewel in her crown of womanhood?"

"Does Mrs. De Lisle know her views on this subject?" he asked.

"Yes."

A quick flush mantled Hendrickson's face.

"Well, what are they?" He questioned eagerly, and in a husky voice.

"She reads the law in Matthew and in Luke, literally."

"The cup is indeed broken, and the precious wine spilled!" exclaimed the unhappy man, rising in strong agitation.

"Paul," said Mrs. Denison, after this agitation had in a measure passed away; "all this I can well understand to be very hard for one who has been so patient, so true, so long suffering. But think calmly; and then ask yourself this question: Would you be willing to marry Jessie Loring while she holds her present views?"

Hendrickson bent his head to think.

"She believes," said Mrs. Denison, "that such a marriage would be adulterous. I put the matter before you in its plainest shape. Now, my friend, are you prepared to take a woman for your wife who is ready to come to you on such terms? I think not. No, not even if her name be Jessie Loring."

"I thank you, my friend, for setting me completely right," said Hendrickson. He spoke sadly, yet with the firmness of a true man. "I have now but one favor to ask. Learn from her own lips, if possible, her real sentiments on this subject."

"I will do so."

"Without delay?"

"Yes. To-morrow I will see Mrs. De Lisle, and confer with her on the subject, and then at the earliest practical moment call with her upon Jessie."

Two days afterwards, Mr. Hendrickson received a note from his friend, asking him to call.

"You have seen her?"

The young man was paler than usual, but calm. His voice was not eagerly expectant, but rather veiled with sadness, as if he had weighed all the chances in his favor, and made up his mind for the worst.

"I have," replied Mrs. Denison.

"She is much changed, I presume?"

"I would scarcely have known her," was answered.

"In what is she changed?"

"She has been growing less of the earth earthy, in all these years of painful discipline. You see this in her changed exterior; your ear perceives it in the tones of her voice; your mind answers to it in the pure sentiments that breathe from her lips. Her very presence gives an atmosphere of heavenly tranquillity."

It was some moments before Hendrickson made further remark. He then said:

"How long a time were you with her, Mrs. Denison?"

"We spent over an hour in her company."

"Was my name mentioned?"

"No."

"Nor the subject in which I feel so deep an interest?"

"Yes, we spoke of that!"

"And you were not in error as to her decision of the case?"

Hendrickson manifested no excitement.

"I was not."

He dropped his eyes again to the floor, and sat musing for some time.

"She does not consider herself free to marry again?"

He looked up with a calm face.

"No."

There was a sigh; a falling of the eyes; and a long, quiet silence.

"I was prepared for it, my friend," he said, speaking almost mournfully. "Since our last interview, I have thought on this subject a great deal, and looked at it from another point of vision. I hare imagined myself in her place, and then pondered the Record. It seemed more imperative. I could not go past it, and yet regard myself innocent, or pure. It seemed a hard saying - but it was said. The mountain was impassable. And so I came fortified for her decision."

"Would you have had it otherwise?" Mrs. Denison asked.

Hendrickson did not answer at once. The question evidently disturbed him.

"The heart is very weak," he said at length.

"But virtue is strong as another Samson," Mrs. Denison spoke quickly.

"Her decision does not produce a feeling of alienation. I am not angry. She stands, it is true, higher up and further off, invested with saintly garments. If she is purer, I must be worthier. I can only draw near in spirit - and there can be no spiritual nearness without a likeness of quality. If the stain of earth is not to be found on her vesture, mine must be white as snow."

"It is by fire we are purified, my friend," answered Mrs. Denison, speaking with unusual feeling.

Not many weeks after this interview with Mrs. Denison, she

received a communication from Hendrickson that filled her with painful surprise. It ran thus:

"MY BEST FRIEND: - When this comes into your hands, I shall be away from B -. It is possible that I may never return again. I do not take this step hastily, but after deep reflection, and in the firm conviction that I am right. If I remain, the probabilities are that I shall meet Jessie Loring, who will come forth gradually from her seclusion; and I am not strong enough, nor cold enough for that. Nor do I think our meeting would make the stream of her life more placed. It has run in wild waves long enough - the waters have been turbid long enough - and mine is not the hand to swirl it with a single eddy. No - no. My love, I trust, is of purer essence. I would bless, not curse - brighten, not cloud the horizon of her life.

"And so I recede as she comes forth into the open day, and shall hide myself from her sight. As she advances by self denials and holy charities towards celestial purity, may I advance also, fast enough at least not to lose sight of her in the far off distance.

"You will meet her often, from this time, dear, true, faithful friend! And I pray you to keep my memory green in her heart. Not with such bold reference as shall disturb its tranquil life. Oh, do not give her pain! But with gentle insinuations; so that the thought of me have no chance to die. I will keep unspotted from the world; yet will I not withdraw myself, but manfully take my place and do battle for the right.

"And now, best of friends, farewell! I go out into the great world, to be absorbed from observation in the crowd. But my heart will remain among the old places, and beat ever faithful to its early loves.

"PAUL HENDRICKSON."

He had withdrawn himself from all business connections, and sold his property. With his small fortune, realized by active, intelligent industry, and now represented by Certificates of Deposit in three of the city banks, he vanished from among those who had known and respected him for years, and left not a sign of the direction he had taken. Even idle rumor, so usually unjust, did him no wrong. He had been, in all his actions, too true a man for even suspicion to touch his name.

CHAPTER XXVII

AS Hendrickson had rightly supposed, Jessie Loring came forth from her seclusion of years. Not all at once, but by gradual intrusions upon the social life around her. At first she went abroad on a mission of charity. Then her friend Mrs. De Lisle, drew her to her house, and there a new face that interested her awakened a new impulse in her mind. And so the work went on, and ere long she was in part restored to society. But how different from the one who had withdrawn from it years before! Suffering and discipline had left upon her their unmistakable signs. The old beauty of countenance had departed. The elegant style - the abounding grace of manner - the fascinating speech - all were gone. Only those to whom she had been most familiar, recognized in the pale, serene countenance, retiring grace and gentle speech of Jessie Loring, the once brilliant Mrs. Dexter.

And quite as different was the effect she produced upon those who came within the sphere of her chastened thoughts. Before, all admired her; now, all who could draw close enough, found in her speech an inspiration to good deeds. Some were wiser - all were better in right purposes - who met her in familiar intercourse. And the more intimately she was known, the more apparent became the higher beauty into which she had arisen; a celestial beauty, that gave angelic lustre at times to her countenance.

To no one did she mention the name of Hendrickson. If she missed him from the circles which had again opened to receive her, none knew that her eyes had ever looked for his presence. No one spoke to her of him, and so she remained for a time in ignorance of his singular disappearance. A caution from Mrs. De Lisle to Mrs. Loring, made that not over-cautious individual prudent in this case.

One day Jessie was visiting Mrs. Denison, to whom she had become warmly attached. She did not show her accustomed cheerfulness, and to the inquiries of Mrs. Denison as to whether she was as well as usual, replied, as it seemed to that lady, evasively. At length she said, with a manner that betrayed a deep interest in the subject:

"I heard a strange story yesterday about an old acquaintance whom I have missed - Mr. Hendrickson."

"What have you heard?" was inquired.

"That he left the city in a mysterious manner several months ago, and has not been heard of since."

"It is true," said Mrs. Denison.

"Was there anything wrong in his conduct?" asked Jessie Loring, her usually pale face showing the warmer hues of feeling.

"Nothing. Not even the breath of suspicion has touched his good name."

"What is the explanation?"

"Common rumor is singularly at fault in the case," replied Mrs. Denison. "I have heard no reason assigned that to me had any appearance of truth."

"Had he failed in business?" asked Miss Loring.

"No. He was in a good business, and accumulating property.

T.S. Arthur

But he sold out, and converting all that he was worth into money, took it with him, and left only his memory behind."

"Had he trouble with any one?"

"No."

Jessie looked concerned - almost sad.

"I would like to know the reason." She spoke partly to herself.

"I alone am in possession of the reason," said Mrs. Denison, after a silence of more than a minute.

"You!"

Thrown off her guard, Jessie spoke eagerly and with surprise.

"Yes. He wrote me a letter at the time, stating in the clearest terms the causes which led to so strange a course of conduct.

"Did you approve of his reasons?" Miss Loring had regained much of her usual calm exterior.

"I accepted them," was answered. "Under all the circumstances of the case, his course was probably the wisest that could have been taken."

"Are you at liberty to state the reasons?" asked Miss Loring.

Mrs. Denison thought for some time.

"Do you desire to hear them?" she then asked, looking steadily into the face of her visitor.

"I do," was firmly answered.

"Then I will place his letter to me in your hands. But not now. When you leave, it will be time enough. You must read it alone."

A sudden gleam shot across the face of Jessie. But it died like a transient meteor.

"I will return home now, Mrs. Denison," she said, with a manner that showed a great deal of suppressed feeling. "You will excuse me, of course."

"Cannot you remain longer? I shall regret your going," said her kind friend.

"Not in my present state of mind. I can see from your manner that I have an interest in the contents of that letter, and I am impatient to know them."

It was all in vain that Jessie Loring sought to calm her feelings as she returned homeward with the letter of Paul Hendrickson held tightly in her hand. The suspense was too much for her. On entering the house of her aunt, she went with unusual haste to her own room, and without waiting to lay aside any of her attire, sat down and opened the letter. There was scarcely a sign of life while she read, so motionless did she sit, as if pulsation were stilled. After reading it to the last word she commenced folding up the letter, but her hands, that showed a slight tremor in the beginning, shook so violently before she was done, that the half closed sheet rattled like a leaf in the wind. Then tears gushed over the letter, falling upon it like rain.

There was no effort on the part of Jessie to repress this wild rush of feeling. Her heart had its own way for a time. In the deep hush that followed, she bowed herself, and kneeled reverently, lifting a sad face and tear-filled eyes upwards with her spirit towards Heaven. She did not ask for strength or comfort - she did not even ask for herself anything. Her soul's deep sympathies were all for another, towards whom a long cherished love had suddenly blazed up, revealing the hidden fires. But she prayed that at all times, in all places, and under all circumstances, *he* might be kept pure.

"Give him," she pleaded, "patient endurance and undying hope. Oh, make his fortitude like the rock, but his humanities yielding and all pervading as the summer airs laden with sweetness. Sustain him by the divine power of truth. Let Thy Word be a staff in his hand when travel-worn, and a sword when the enemy seeks his life. In his own strength he cannot walk in this way; in his own strength he cannot battle with his foes - but in Thy strength he will be strong as a lion, and as invincible as an army."

After rising from her knees, Miss Loring, over whose spirit a deep quietude had fallen, re-opened Hendrickson's letter and read it again; and not once only but many times, until every word and sentence were written on her memory.

"The way may be rough, and our feet not well shod for the long journey," she said, almost with a smile on her pure face, "the sky may be sunless and moonless, and thick clouds may hide even the stars - but there are soft green meadows beyond, and glorious sunshine. If I am not to meet him here, I shall be gathered lovingly into his arms there, and God will bless the union!"

When next Mrs. Denison saw this young martyr, there was even a serener aspect in her countenance than before. She was in possession of a secret that gave a new vitality to her existence. Until now, all in regard to Hendrickson had been vague and uncertain. Their few brief but disastrous meetings had only revealed an undying interest; but as to the quality of his love, his sentiments in regard to her, and his principles of life, she knew literally nothing. Now all was made clear; and her soul grew strong within her as she looked forward into the distance.

"I will keep that letter," she said to Mrs. Denison, in so firm a voice that her friend was surprised. "It is more really addressed to me than it is to you; and it was but fair that it should come into my possession. He is one of earth's nobler spirits."

"You say well, Miss Loring. He is one of earth's nobler spirits. I know him. How he would stand the fire, I could not tell. But I had faith in him; and my faith was but a prophecy. He has come out purified. I was not at first satisfied with this last step; but on close reflection, I am inclined to the belief that he was right. I do not think either of you are strong enough yet to meet. You would be drawn together by an attraction that might obscure your higher perceptions, and lead you to break over all impediments. That, with your views, would not be well. There would be a cloud in the sky of your happiness; a spot on your marriage garments; a shadow on your consciences."

"There would - there would!" replied Miss Loring with sudden feeling. Then, as the current grew placid again, she said:

"I can hardly make you comprehend the change which that letter has wrought in me. All the thick clouds that mantled my sky, have lifted themselves from the horizon, showing bright gleams of the far away blue; and sunrays are streaming down by a hundred rifts. Oh, this knowledge that I am so deeply, purely, faithfully loved, trammelled as I am, and forbidden to marry, fills my soul with happiness inexpressible. We shall be, when the hand of our wise and good Father leads us together, and His smile falls unclouded upon our union, more blessed a thousand fold than if, in the eagerness of natural impulses, we had let our feelings have sway."

"If you are both strong enough, you will have the higher blessing," was the only answer made by Mrs. Denison.

From that period a change in Jessie Loring was visible to all eyes. There came into her countenance a warmer hue of health; her bearing was more erect, yet not self-confident; her eyes were brighter, and occasionally the flash of old-time thought was in them. Everywhere she went, she attracted; and all who came into familiar intercourse with her, felt the sweetness of her lovely character. The secret of this change was known to but few, and they kept it sacred. Not even Mrs. Loring, the good-hearted aunt, who loved her with a mother's maternal fondness, was admitted into her confidence, for she felt that mere worldliness would bruise her heart by contact. But the change, though its causes were not seen, was perceived as something to love, by Aunt Phoebe, who felt for her niece a daily increasing attachment.

And so the weeks moved on; and so the years came and went. Little change was seen in Jessie Loring; except, that the smile which had been restored, gradually grew less, though it did not bear away the heavenly sweetness from her countenance. In all true charities that came within her sphere of action, whether the ministration were to bodily necessities, or moral needs, she was an angel of mercy; and few met her in life's daily walk, but had occasion to think of her as one living very near the sources of Divine love.

CHAPTER XXVIII

TEN years had glided away, yet not in all that time had Jessie Loring received a word of intelligence from Paul Hendrickson. He had passed from sight like a ship when darkness falls upon the ocean - the morning sees her not again, and the billows give no record of the way she went. But still Jessie bore his image at her heart; still her love was undimmed, and her confidence unshaken - and still she felt herself bound by the old shackles, which no human hand could break from her fettered limbs.

One day, about this time, as Mrs. Denison sat reading, a servant came into her room and handing her a card, said:

"There is a gentleman waiting in the parlor to see you."

She looked at the card, and started with surprise. It bore the name of PAUL HENDRICKSON.

"My dear friend!" she exclaimed, grasping both of his hands, as she stood facing him a few moments afterwards.

"My best friend!" was the simple response, but in a voice tremulous with feeling.

A little while they stood, gazing curiously yet with affectionate interest, into each other's face.

"You are not much changed; and nothing for the worse," said

T.S. Arthur

Mrs. Denison.

"And you wear the countenance of yesterday," he replied, almost fondly. "How many thousands of times since we parted, have I desired to stand looking into your eyes as I do now! Dear friend! my heart has kept your memory fresh as spring's first offerings."

"Where have you been, in all these years of absence?" Mrs. Denison asked, as they sat down, still holding each other's hands tightly.

"Far away from here; but of that hereafter. You have already guessed the meaning of my return to the old places."

"No."

"What! Have you not heard of Mr. Dexter's decease?"

"Paul! is that so?" Mrs. Denison was instantly excited.

"It is. I had the information from a correspondent in London, who sent me a paper in which was a brief obituary. He died nearly three months ago, of fever contracted in a hospital, where he had gone to visit the captain of one of his vessels, just arrived from the coast of Africa. The notice speaks of him as an American gentleman of wealth and great respectability."

"And the name is Leon Dexter?" said Mrs. Denison.

"Yes. There is no question as to the identity. And now, my good friend, what of Jessie Loring? I pray you keep me not longer in suspense."

So wholly absorbed were they, that the ringing of the street door bell had not been heard, nor the movement of the servant along the passage. Ere Mrs. Denison could reply, the parlor door was pushed quietly open, and Miss Loring entered.

"She stands before you!" said Mrs. Denison, starting up and advancing a step or two.

"Jessie Loring!"

Mr. Hendrickson uttered the name slowly, but in a voice touched with the profoundest emotion. He had arisen, but did not advance. She stood suddenly still, and held her breath, while a paleness overspread her features. But her long training had given her great self-control.

"Mr. Hendrickson," she said, advancing across the room.

He grasped her hand, but she did not return the ardent pressure, though the touch went thrilling to her heart. But the paleness had left her face.

At this moment Mrs. Denison came forward, and covering their clasped hands with hers, said in a low, but very emphatic voice:

"There is no impediment! God has removed the last obstruction, and your way is plain."

Instantly the whole frame of Miss Loring seemed jarred as by a heavy stroke; and she would have fallen through weakness, if Hendrickson had not thrown an arm around her. Bearing her to a sofa, he laid her, very tenderly, in a reclining position, with her head resting against Mrs. Denison. But he kept one of her hands tightly within his own; and she made no effort to withdraw it.

"There is no obstruction now, dear friends," resumed Mrs. Denison. "The long agony is over - the sad error corrected. The patience of hope, the fidelity of love, the martyr-spirit that could bear torture, yet not swerve from its integrity, are all to find their exceeding great reward. I did not look for it so soon. Far in advance of the present I saw the long road each had to travel, still stretching its weary length. But suddenly the pilgrimage has ended. The goal is won while yet the sun stands at full meridian - while yet the feet are strong, and the heart brave for endurance or battle. Heroes are ye, and this is my greeting!"

With eyes still closed, Jessie lay very still upon the bosom of this dear friend. But oh, what a revelation of joy was in the sweet, half-formed smile that arched her lips with beauty! Hendrickson stood, still grasping her hand, and looking down into her pure, tranquil face, with such a rapture pervading his soul, that he seemed as if entering upon the felicities of heaven.

"This is even better than my hopes," he said, speaking at length, but in a subdued voice.

Jessie opened her eyes, and now gazed at him calmly, but lovingly. What a manly presence was his! How wonderfully he was changed! - Thought, suffering, endurance, virtue, honor, had all been at work upon his face, cutting away the earthly and the sensual, until only the lines of that imperishable beauty which is of the spirit, remained. Every well-remembered feature was there; but the expression of his whole face was new.

A moment or two only did she look at him - but she read a volume in love's history at a glance - then closed her eyes again, and, as she did so, gave back to the hand that still held hers, an answering pressure.

The long, long trial of faith, love and high religious principle was over, and they were now standing at the open door of blessing.

And so the reward came at last, as come it always does, to the true, the faithful, the pure, and the loving - if not in this world, assuredly in the next - and the great error of their lives stood corrected.

But what a lesson for the heart! Oh, is there a more fearful consummation of error in the beginning of life than a wholly discordant marriage! This mating of higher and lower natures - of delicacy with coarseness - of sensuality with almost spiritual refinement - of dove-like meekness with falcon cruelty - of the lamb with the bear! It makes the very heart bleed to think of the undying anguish that is all around us, springing from this most frightful cause of misery!

In less than a month Paul Hendrickson again departed from B -, but this time not alone, nor with his destination involved in mystery. His second self went with him, and their faces were turned towards a southern island, where the earth was as rich in blossom and verdure as the bride's heart in undying love. Here his home had been for years; and here his name was an honored word among the people - synonymous with manly integrity, Christian virtue, and true benevolence.

After the long, fierce battle, peace had come with its tranquil blessings. After the storm, the sunshine had fallen in glorious beauty. After the night of suffering, morning had broken in joy.

We stand and gaze, with rapt interest, upon the river when it leaps wildly over the cataract, or sweeps foaming down perilous rapids, or rushes through mountain gorges; but turn away from its quiet beauty when it glides pleasantly along through green savannahs. Such is our interest in life. And so we drop the curtain, and close our history here.

Choose from Thousands of 1stWorldLibrary Classics By

A. M. Barnard
Ada Leverson
Adolphus William Ward
Aesop
Agatha Christie
Alexander Aaronsohn
Alexander Kielland
Alexandre Dumas
Alfred Gatty
Alfred Ollivant
Alice Duer Miller
Alice Turner Curtis
Alice Dunbar
Allen Chapman
Ambrose Bierce
Amelia E. Barr
Amory H. Bradford
Andrew Lang
Andrew McFarland Davis
Andy Adams
Anna Alice Chapin
Anna Sewell
Annie Besant
Annie Hamilton Donnell
Annie Payson Call
Annie Roe Carr
Annonaymous
Anton Chekhov
Arnold Bennett
Arthur Conan Doyle
Arthur M. Winfield
Arthur Ransome
Arthur Schnitzler
Atticus
B.H. Baden-Powell
B. M. Bower
B. C. Chatterjee
Baroness Emmuska Orczy
Baroness Orczy
Basil King
Bayard Taylor
Ben Macomber
Bertha Muzzy Bower
Bjornstjerne Bjornson
Booth Tarkington
Boyd Cable
Bram Stoker
C. Collodi
C. E. Orr

C. M. Ingleby
Carolyn Wells
Catherine Parr Traill
Charles A. Eastman
Charles Amory Beach
Charles Dickens
Charles Dudley Warner
Charles Farrar Browne
Charles Ives
Charles Kingsley
Charles Klein
Charles Hanson Towne
Charles Lathrop Pack
Charles Romyn Dake
Charles Whibley
Charles Willing Beale
Charlotte M. Braeme
Charlotte M. Yonge
Charlotte Perkins Stetson
Clair W. Hayes
Clarence Day Jr.
Clarence E. Mulford
Clemence Housman
Confucius
Coningsby Dawson
Cornelis DeWitt Wilcox
Cyril Burleigh
D. H. Lawrence
Daniel Defoe
David Garnett
Dinah Craik
Don Carlos Janes
Donald Keyhoe
Dorothy Kilner
Dougan Clark
Douglas Fairbanks
E. Nesbit
E.P.Roe
E. Phillips Oppenheim
Earl Barnes
Edgar Rice Burroughs
Edith Van Dyne
Edith Wharton
Edward Everett Hale
Edward J. O'Biren
Edward S. Ellis
Edwin L. Arnold
Eleanor Atkins
Eliot Gregory

Elizabeth Gaskell
Elizabeth McCracken
Elizabeth Von Arnim
Ellem Key
Emerson Hough
Emilie F. Carlen
Emily Dickinson
Enid Bagnold
Enilor Macartney Lane
Erasmus W. Jones
Ernie Howard Pie
Ethel May Dell
Ethel Turner
Ethel Watts Mumford
Eugenie Foa
Eugene Wood
Eustace Hale Ball
Evelyn Everett-green
Everard Cotes
F. H. Cheley
F. J. Cross
F. Marion Crawford
Federick Austin Ogg
Ferdinand Ossendowski
Francis Bacon
Francis Darwin
Frances Hodgson Burnett
Frances Parkinson Keyes
Frank Gee Patchin
Frank Harris
Frank Jewett Mather
Frank L. Packard
Frank V. Webster
Frederic Stewart Isham
Frederick Trevor Hill
Frederick Winslow Taylor
Friedrich Kerst
Friedrich Nietzsche
Fyodor Dostoyevsky
G.A. Henty
G.K. Chesterton
Gabrielle E. Jackson
Garrett P. Serviss
Gaston Leroux
George A. Warren
George Ade
Geroge Bernard Shaw
George Durston
George Ebers

George Eliot
George Gissing
George MacDonald
George Meredith
George Orwell
George Sylvester Viereck
George Tucker
George W. Cable
George Wharton James
Gertrude Atherton
Gordon Casserly
Grace E. King
Grace Gallatin
Grace Greenwood
Grant Allen
Guillermo A. Sherwell
Gulielma Zollinger
Gustav Flaubert
H. A. Cody
H. B. Irving
H.C. Bailey
H. G. Wells
H. H. Munro
H. Irving Hancock
H. Rider Haggard
H. W. C. Davis
Haldeman Julius
Hall Caine
Hamilton Wright Mabie
Hans Christian Andersen
Harold Avery
Harold McGrath
Harriet Beecher Stowe
Harry Castlemon
Harry Coghill
Harry Houidini
Hayden Carruth
Helent Hunt Jackson
Helen Nicolay
Hendrik Conscience
Hendy David Thoreau
Henri Barbusse
Henrik Ibsen
Henry Adams
Henry Ford
Henry Frost
Henry James
Henry Jones Ford
Henry Seton Merriman
Henry W Longfellow
Herbert A. Giles

Herbert Carter
Herbert N. Casson
Herman Hesse
Hildegard G. Frey
Homer
Honore De Balzac
Horace B. Day
Horace Walpole
Horatio Alger Jr.
Howard Pyle
Howard R. Garis
Hugh Lofting
Hugh Walpole
Humphry Ward
Ian Maclaren
Inez Haynes Gillmore
Irving Bacheller
Isabel Hornibrook
Israel Abrahams
Ivan Turgenev
J.G.Austin
J. Henri Fabre
J. M. Barrie
J. Macdonald Oxley
J. S. Fletcher
J. S. Knowles
J. Storer Clouston
Jack London
Jacob Abbott
James Allen
James Andrews
James Baldwin
James Branch Cabell
James DeMille
James Joyce
James Lane Allen
James Lane Allen
James Oliver Curwood
James Oppenheim
James Otis
James R. Driscoll
Jane Austen
Jane L. Stewart
Janet Aldridge
Jens Peter Jacobsen
Jerome K. Jerome
John Burroughs
John Cournos
John F. Kennedy
John Gay
John Glasworthy

John Habberton
John Joy Bell
John Kendrick Bangs
John Milton
John Philip Sousa
Jonas Lauritz Idemil Lie
Jonathan Swift
Joseph A. Altsheler
Joseph Carey
Joseph Conrad
Joseph E. Badger Jr
Joseph Hergesheimer
Joseph Jacobs
Jules Vernes
Julian Hawthrone
Julie A Lippmann
Justin Huntly McCarthy
Kakuzo Okakura
Kenneth Grahame
Kenneth McGaffey
Kate Langley Bosher
Kate Langley Bosher
Katherine Cecil Thurston
Katherine Stokes
L. A. Abbot
L. T. Meade
L. Frank Baum
Latta Griswold
Laura Dent Crane
Laura Lee Hope
Laurence Housman
Lawrence Beasley
Leo Tolstoy
Leonid Andreyev
Lewis Carroll
Lewis Sperry Chafer
Lilian Bell
Lloyd Osbourne
Louis Hughes
Louis Tracy
Louisa May Alcott
Lucy Fitch Perkins
Lucy Maud Montgomery
Luther Benson
Lydia Miller Middleton
Lyndon Orr
M. Corvus
M. H. Adams
Margaret E. Sangster
Margret Howth
Margaret Vandercook

Margret Penrose	Rex E. Beach	Thomas H. Huxley
Maria Edgeworth	Richard Harding Davis	Thomas Hardy
Maria Thompson Daviess	Richard Jefferies	Thomas More
Mariano Azuela	Richard Le Gallienne	Thornton W. Burgess
Marion Polk Angellotti	Robert Barr	U. S. Grant
Mark Overton	Robert Frost	Valentine Williams
Mark Twain	Robert Gordon Anderson	Various Authors
Mary Austin	Robert L. Drake	Vaughan Kester
Mary Catherine Crowley	Robert Lansing	Victor Appleton
Mary Cole	Robert Lynd	Victoria Cross
Mary Hastings Bradley	Robert Michael Ballantyne	Virginia Woolf
Mary Roberts Rinehart	Robert W. Chambers	Wadsworth Camp
Mary Rowlandson	Rosa Nouchette Carey	Walter Camp
M. Wollstonecraft Shelley	Rudyard Kipling	Walter Scott
Maud Lindsay	Samuel B. Allison	Washington Irving
Max Beerbohm	Samuel Hopkins Adams	Wilbur Lawton
Myra Kelly	Sarah Bernhardt	Wilkie Collins
Nathaniel Hawthrone	Sarah C. Hallowell	Willa Cather
Nicolo Machiavelli	Selma Lagerlof	Willard F. Baker
O. F. Walton	Sherwood Anderson	William Dean Howells
Oscar Wilde	Sigmund Freud	William le Queux
Owen Johnson	Standish O'Grady	W. Makepeace Thackeray
P.G. Wodehouse	Stanley Weyman	William W. Walter
Paul and Mabel Thorne	Stella Benson	William Shakespeare
Paul G. Tomlinson	Stella M. Francis	Winston Churchill
Paul Severing	Stephen Crane	Yei Theodora Ozaki
Percy Brebner	Stewart Edward White	Yogi Ramacharaka
Peter B. Kyne	Stijn Streuvels	Young E. Allison
Plato	Swami Abhedananda	Zane Grey
R. Derby Holmes	Swami Parmananda	
R. L. Stevenson	T. S. Ackland	
R. S. Ball	T. S. Arthur	
Rabindranath Tagore	The Princess Der Ling	
Rahul Alvares	Thomas A. Janvier	
Ralph Bonehill	Thomas A Kempis	
Ralph Henry Barbour	Thomas Anderton	
Ralph Victor	Thomas Bailey Aldrich	
Ralph Waldo Emmerson	Thomas Bulfinch	
Rene Descartes	Thomas De Quincey	
Rex Beach	Thomas Dixon